THE ESL
SAFETY BOOK

THE ESL
SAFETY BOOK

Craig Dougherty
&
Robert Emigh

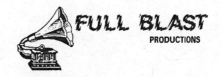

FULL BLAST
PRODUCTIONS

Copyright © 2001 FULL BLAST Productions

IN CANADA   IN THE UNITED STATES

FB Productions   FB Productions
Box 408   Box 1297
Virgil, Ontario   Lewiston, New York 14092-8297
L0S 1T0

Phone: 905-468-7558
Fax: 905-468-5706
E-mail: fbp@vaxxine.com
Website: www.fullblastproductions.com

National Library of Canada Cataloguing in Publication Data

Dougherty, Craig
    The ESL safety book

ISBN 1-895451-39-6

1. English Language -- Textbooks for second language learners.
2. Readers--Safety education. I. Emigh, Robert, 1955-   .   II. Title.

PE1128.D68 2000   428.2' 4   C2001-902960-8

Printed in Canada.

ISBN 1-895451-39-6

Table of Contents

INTRODUCTION

THE ESL SAFETY BOOK is a reproducible ESL/EFL/LITERACY reading-and-discussion text for beginners in English. It offers a number of important design features to make both teaching and learning easier and more enjoyable.

1) Contextualized learning: The short self-contained articles in each unit benefit from a very clear focus that facilitates realistic concentration on inter-related items of vocabulary and grammar that are relevant to the topic and the argumentative purpose.

2) Content that really matters: Each unit examines an element of safety that will genuinely interest and inform your students.

3) Lively journalistic style: Although the passages are carefully limited to an elementary level of language difficulty, their style remains vivid and authentic.

4) Well-balanced exercises: The exercises offer a good range of activities for each unit, including: multiple choice, getting the main idea, basic comprehension, remembering details, inferences, true or false, matching, vocabulary study, dictionary practice, cause and effect, cloze exercises summarizing information, statistics, chronology, minimal pairs, context clues, discussion questions and more.

5) Illustrations: There is a clear and evocative illustration in each unit; this can be used as a pre-reading exercise, for vocabulary brainstorming, or as the basis for discussion.

6) Answer Key: The text includes a full answer key for every closed-ended question in every unit.

7) Reproducible: Photocopying rights are granted to the individual teacher or the single school purchasing the materials. A copy of this book purchased by an individual teacher is that teacher's property and can travel with her from school to school. A single copy of this book may not be kept at a resource center and used to service several schools. To be entitled to copy this book, a teacher in the school or the school itself must own an original copy. Please respect copyright.

This package can be used quite simply as it is presented in these pages. In fact, it was carefully planned to be effective in that way. However, resourceful teachers will most likely want to consider one or more of the following suggestions:

- Pre-Activity: Instead of immediately beginning to read the passage, have students start with a discussion or game to encourage thought about the theme or content of the unit. The picture or title at the head of the unit can be useful in this connection; so can newspaper or magazine illustrations or headlines, or current television or radio news items.

- Order of Exercises: By all means, use all the activities provided for each unit, and allow sufficient time for these to be completed thoroughly (including time for small groups to discuss alternate answers and so on). But build in variety by changing the order in which the exercises are done, and by varying the designation of activities for in-class or at-home assignment.

- Intensity of Work: Be sure to take full advantage of the wide range of different kinds of involvement that these materials offer. For instance, students can be urged to research topics further. In many libraries books, newspapers, videos, compact discs and other things can be found relating to these subjects. Or, to take another approach, the teacher can bring the related materials to the classroom.

- Post-Activity: Once the class has finished the set of exercises in the text itself, think about rounding off the cycle with a post-activity that clearly links the book and the schoolroom to the wider world. Learners might pursue the theme or content of a given unit by making a bulletin-board collage of their own art work and/or comments, writing letters to a relevant person or institution, going on a visit, watching a video...you will find many ways to reinforce the vocabulary, grammar and content one more time while you also build the self-image of learners as competent language-users for real-life purposes.

- Flexibility: There is no problem with using these units just as provided, but in many circumstances their best application will be as a flexible data-base of content-centered readings that you can access as you see fit, to tap into the energy of learners' natural curiosity about such passing interests as news items, current movies, new music, or extra-curricular activities. Dip into this treasure-trove of self-contained units to find the exact passage to exploit a "hot topic." Each term, you'll have different students with different experiences, and so your use of the text will differ as well. With this flexible resource, you can change to meet your students' needs!

Insect Bites

Many scientists believe that there are more than 2 million different kinds of insects. Some insects help humans by eating decaying things and helping to produce medicines and cloth. However, there are other insects that carry dangerous diseases. Also, there are people who are allergic to certain types of insect stings or bites.

Two of the most dangerous insects are mosquitoes and ticks. Mosquitoes carry dangerous diseases like the Malaria and West Nile viruses while ticks carry Lyme disease. The best way to avoid mosquito and tick bites is to wear long sleeves and pants and to use insect repellent. It is also a good idea to stay inside during the early evening to avoid mosquitoes and to wear light colored clothes to make it easier to find ticks on your body. Remember that you may not feel a mosquito or tick bite. A fever and chills are symptoms of Malaria and West Nile viruses. A red rash is a sign of Lyme disease. If you notice any of these signs after being outside, go to a doctor.

When any insect bites or stings, wash the area with soap and water. Try not to rub or scratch it. If you have problems breathing or become dizzy, you may be allergic to the sting or bite. Go to a doctor or hospital immediately.

Nature is very interesting to explore but always respect the creatures that live there and be prepared to protect yourself.

Multiple Choice

1. If you feel chills and have a fever after a mosquito bites, you should...

    a) scratch it.
    b) do not worry about it.
    c) see a doctor.

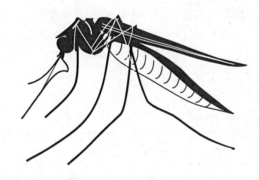

2. To avoid mosquitoes and ticks, you should...

    a) go out in the early evening.
    b) wear dark clothes.
    c) wear insect repellant.

3. If a person has problems breathing after an insect bite or sting...

    a) do not worry about it.
    b) look for the insect.
    c) see a doctor immediately.

Sentence Completions

Complete each sentence below.

1. When an insect bites or stings _____

2. Many scientists believe _____

Common and Proper Nouns

There are 2 kinds of nouns: common and proper.

Common nouns are general and do not have capital letters unless they begin a sentence:

humans, mosquitoes, soap, etc.

Proper nouns are a specific name or title and are always capitalized:

English, Jack, Seattle, etc.

Find 3 examples of common nouns and 3 examples of proper nouns in the article about insect bites. Remember that a common noun may have a capital letter if it begins a sentence.

COMMON NOUNS

1. _____

2. _____

3. _____

PROPER NOUNS

1. _____

2. _____

3. _____

Personal Information

You are sitting at home when someone calls you to say: "Hello! My name is John and I am happy to tell you that you have just won $1 million! Before we send you the cheque, we need to know your Social Security or Social Insurance number, your credit card number, and your bank account information...." There is a famous saying: If something sounds too good to be true, it probably is. In this example, John could be a criminal who wants to use this information to commit a crime against you or someone else.

Be very careful about to who you tell your Social Security or Social Insurance number. With that number, someone with bad intentions may be able to find information about how much money you earn, what kinds of health problems you have, your grades, and many other kinds of important information. When you give out your number, be sure you know the person you are giving it to and that you know how they will use it.

If the wrong people get a hold of your personal information it can cost you a lot of money. If criminals know your bank account number, they may be able to steal any money you have deposited there. Normally, banks tell their clients not to give this number to anyone. Also, be very careful about to who you tell your credit card number, especially if people want you to give it to them by phone or over the Internet. Thieves can even steal your phone card number and charge phone calls to your account.

If you think that a criminal has any of your personal information, call the police immediately. You should also tell your bank or credit card company if you lose your cheques, ATM card, or credit card. Most people are honest and will not try to hurt you. Unfortunately, "most people" does not mean "all people".

The Main Idea

The main idea of this story is...

    a) the famous saying is true.
    b) recognizing criminals.
    c) to be careful about to who you tell your personal information.

Sentence Completions

Conplete each sentence below.

1. It is a bad idea to give your ATM card to a stranger because _____

2. Criminals may want your Social Security/Insurance number for _____

3. If a criminal has your personal information you should _____

Related Words

Find words that are related to the words below:

1. knowledge (a noun) ___ ___ ___ w (a verb)

2. inform (a verb) ___ ___ ___ ___ ___ ___ ___ ___ ___ ___ n (a noun)

3. person (a noun) ___ ___ ___ ___ ___ ___ ___ l (an adjective)

4. care (a verb) ___ ___ ___ ___ ___ ___ l (an adjective)

5. crime (a noun) ___ ___ ___ ___ ___ ___ ___ l (a person)

Adverbs

Adverbs are words that modify verbs, adjectives, or other adverbs. Many times, they end in ñly, but not always. Unscramble the following adverbs. All of them are in the reading.

1. stuj   _____

2. oto   _____

3. ervy   _____

4. larmlyon   _____

5. sola   _____

6. neve   _____

7. emmidailtey _____

4

A.I.D.S./H.I.V.

A.I.D.S. (acquired immunodeficiency syndrome) is caused by a virus that is called H.I.V. (human immunodeficiency virus). H.I.V. was first identified in 1981. The H.I.V. virus makes the body weak so that it is unable to protect itself from serious illnesses. The virus is mostly found in blood, but it may also be found in body fluids, like semen or breast milk.

One of the biggest myths about A.I.D.S. is that it can be passed from one person to another by saliva, tears, sweat or by insect bites. There is no proof of this. H.I.V. is known to be passed from one person to another in one of three ways: 1) sexual intercourse 2) contact with blood 3) from mother to her fetus or baby. Therefore, people can get H.I.V. from unprotected sex or from sharing needles while using drugs; babies can get H.I.V. in the womb or from their mother's milk. You cannot get H.I.V. from someone coughing or sneezing on you; by sharing drinking glasses or from dishes; from touching doorknobs or from mosquito bites.

Although there is no cure for A.I.D.S. at the present time, there is medicine that can slow the disease. It is also very important to remember that you can protect yourself from A.I.D.S. Do not inject drugs into your body. If a person does inject drugs, he or she must use a clean needle. Also, never have unprotected sex. If you do not know your partner well, use a latex condom (other types of condoms are not as effective in stopping the spread of the virus).

Remember that being informed, taking precautions and only having safe sex help stop the spread of A.I.D.S. These things are the best weapons we have to fight this terrible disease.

Multiple Choice

1. The H.I.V. virus is found mostly in...

    a) saliva.
    b) blood.
    c) sweat.

2. You can get the H.I.V. virus from...

    a) someone coughing on you.
    b) mosquitoes.
    c) unprotected sex.

3. The best ways to fight A.I.D.S./H.I.V. are...

    a) by not sharing drinking glasses or dishes.
    b) by not touching or shaking hands with strangers.
    c) through education and practicing safe sex.

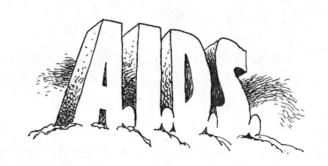

Summarizing Information

Choose the best summary for each paragraph. Put summary letters in the correct spaces. Of the six summaries, only four (4) can be used.

Paragraph 1 talks about _____

Paragraph 2 talks about _____

Paragraph 3 talks about _____

Paragraph 4 talks about _____

a) How to avoid contracting A.I.D.S.

b) The cure for A.I.D.S.

c) Myths and truths about contracting the disease.

d) The best kind of condoms.

e) Definitions of A.I.D.S. and H.I.V.

f) The best ways to fight A.I.D.S.

Discussion Questions

1. Think back to when you first heard about the A.I.D.S. disease. What do you know now about the disease that you did not know then? How much have we learned about the disease in the past few years?

2. A few years ago, it was announced that Earvin "Magic" Johnson, a famous American basketball player, had contracted H.I.V.. Do you think that that announcement changed the way people thought about the disease? Why or why not?

3. Imagine that you found out that a classmate of yours had H.I.V. Do you think that it would change the relationship you and that classmate have? Why or why not?

Asthma And Children

Asthma is a serious lung disease that causes breathing problems. These breathing problems are called attacks. The attacks can be mild to moderate or they can be severe. In severe attacks, the patient finds it very difficult to breathe and may also have trouble talking. The lips and fingernails may turn blue or gray. In a severe attack, the patient must take his or her asthma medicine and then immediately see a doctor. In less severe attacks, the patient should take the asthma medicine; if the medicine does not work, the patient should call a doctor.

People of all ages can get asthma, but the greatest increases of asthma cases in recent years have been among young people. Over 5 million people in North America under the age of 18 have asthma: about one in every nine children. Asthma is a very dangerous disease; however, when it is treated properly, it can be controlled. With the proper treatment, children with asthma can live full lives and do all kinds of activities, including exercise and sports.

No one knows exactly what causes asthma. We do know that some special event starts the asthma attack. This is called a trigger. The trigger may be a virus (like a cold), cigarette smoke, exercise, cold air or many other things. The important thing is to find the trigger and then avoid those triggers. Doctors can also prescribe medicine that will make the attack less severe. Remember that asthma can be controlled; the better you and your child understand the disease, the better able you will be to control it.

Multiple Choice

1. The breathing problems a person has when he or she has asthma are called...

   a) lung diseases.
   b) gasps.
   c) attacks.

2. The largest number of new asthma cases have been reported in...

   a) children and young adults.
   b) adults.
   c) old people.

3. When we talk about asthma, a "trigger" means...

   a) a part of a gun.
   b) a dog.
   c) the thing that starts the asthma attack.

Synonyms Or Antonyms?

Look at the two words. Decide if they are synonyms (words that have the same meaning) or antonyms (words that have the opposite meaning).

1. serious   severe   synonym / antonym

2. properly   correctly   synonym / antonym

3. increase   decrease   synonym / antonym

4. recently   lately   synonym / antonym

5. full   empty   synonym / antonym

Discussion Question

Over the last twenty years, the number of asthma cases in the North America has doubled. Can you think of any reasons why this is happening?

Drinking Water Safety

Every human must drink water to survive. Unfortunately, not all water is safe to drink. Sometimes even water from your taps at home may not be safe to drink. If water looks cloudy or has a strange smell, be sure it is safe before you drink it. Water can be especially risky when it contains lead, microbes, or after a natural disaster has occurred.

Nowadays, lead in water is very rare. However, lead in water can be very dangerous to small children. Lead would enter the water from lead pipes. If you live in a house that was built before 1930 you may have lead pipes so you should have the water tested by your local health department. A doctor can also test a child's blood. Also, it is a good practice to boil cold, not warm or hot, tap water for cooking because warmer water absorbs more lead.

Microbes such as viruses and bacteria are often in water. Most of the time, they do not create serious health problems. Some microbes may cause stomach problems like nausea , vomiting, and diarrhea. If someone has these problems for more than a few days that person should see a doctor.

Probably the time you need to be the most concerned about drinking water is after a natural disaster like a flood or a heavy rainstorm. You should listen for public announcements because these will often inform people if there is a serious health risk. Before you drink water after a disaster, it is a good idea to filter it, boil it, and treat it with chlorine.

Water should be the healthiest liquid we humans drink. Is it too much to ask to have water that tastes good flowing from our taps?

Multiple Choice

1. The main idea of this reading is...

   a) do not drink water.
   b) lead in water is healthy.
   c) possible causes of problems with drinking water.

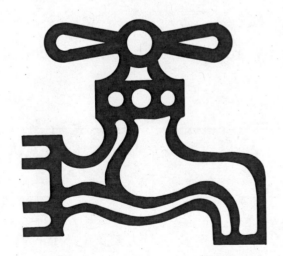

2. You should probably be careful about drinking water...

   a) after a disaster.   b) before a disaster.   c) in modern buildings.

3. If you have young children, you should...

   a) not give them water to drink. b) make sure the water has microbes. c) none of these.

Making Water Safe

List 5 ways found in the reading to make water safer to drink.

1. _____

2. _____

3. _____

4. _____

5. _____

Saying The Letter S Like The Letter Z

English has many words that end in the letter S. However, we do not always pronounce the final S in the same way.

If the letter before the final S is voiced (a,b,d,e,,i,l,m,n,o,r,u,v,y) you say the S with a Z sound.

In the word MicrobeS, you say the letter S like the letter Z. In this example the letter before S is E.

Find 4 words from the reading that end is S but that we pronounce with a Z sound.

1. _____

2. _____

3. _____

4. _____

Bicycles

Bicycles are fun and an excellent form of exercise, but they can also be dangerous. Children and young teenagers are those who are most at risk when riding bicycles. More than 70% of children from 5 to 14 years old ride bicycles. This age group suffers more than 50% of all bicycle-related injuries. The typical accident happens between the months of May and August (55% of all accidents), between 3 p.m. and 6 p.m. (39% of all accidents) and within one mile of the bicyclist's home.

Among children 14 years old and younger, more than 80% of bicycle deaths are due to the bicycle rider's behavior; in particular, riding into a street without stopping, turning left or turning into traffic that is coming from behind, not stopping for a stop sign or riding against traffic.

The single most important safety precaution is for bicycle riders to wear a helmet. Helmets have been shown to reduce the possibility of a head injury by as much as 85%. Unfortunately, many young riders do not wear their helmets. Only 15-20% of North American young people who ride bikes use their helmets and only 11% of children from 11-14 years old use their helmets. Getting every child to wear a helmet is the first and most important step in bicycle riding safety.

Multiple Choice

1. Which of the following is not typical of most bicycle accidents?

    a) They happen near the bicyclist's home.
    b) They happen in the summer time.
    c) They happen in the morning.

2. Which of the following is not an example of behavior that leads to a bicycle accident?

    a) Not obeying the traffic signs.
    b) Stopping before turning into a street.
    c) Riding in the wrong direction in traffic.

3. Which group is most likely to be hurt while riding a bicycle?

    a) Elementary and junior high school students.
    b) High school students.
    c) College students.

Vocabulary

Match the word(s) from the story in Column A with its definition in Column B.

        A   B

1. at risk

                                 a. The way you say and do things.

2. behavior

                                 b. To be hurt.

3. traffic

                                 c. To be in danger.

4. precaution

                                 d. The movement of cars and trucks along a street or road.

5. injury

                                 e. Something you do to prevent or stop something dangerous from happening.

Statistics

The article on bicycles provides many statistics. Complete the following by giving the correct statistic.

1. The percentage of people from 5 to 14 years old who ride bicycles.

_____

2. The percentage that helmets reduce the possibility of a head injury.

_____

3. The percentage of North American young people who use their helmet.

_____

4. The percentage of bicycle accidents that happen between 3 p.m. and 6 p.m.

_____

5. The percentage of cycling accidents for children 14 and under that occur because of the bicyclist's behavior.

_____

Choking

Choking is when you cannot breathe because something has become stuck in your throat. Choking is often the result of attempting to swallowing food that has not been chewed enough. If a person can speak, cough or breathe then he or she is not choking. If you ask the person, "Are you choking?" and they cannot respond, then they probably are choking and you need to take immediate action.

The simplest way to clear someone's throat is by doing a finger sweep. Open the person's mouth and if you can see food stuck in the back of the throat, try to remove it by sweeping your finger around the person's mouth. Be careful not to push the food deeper into the throat. Never do a finger sweep with a child if the food cannot be seen. If the food cannot be removed with a finger sweep, you should try the Heimlich Maneuver, another method for dislodging food that is trapped in someone's throat.

However, the best way to avoid choking is through prevention. Cut food into small pieces and chew it thoroughly. Children should eat at the table and always in a sitting position. Do not feed children under four years old food that may be difficult to chew, such as hot dogs, nuts, large pieces of meat or cheese, whole grapes, hard or sticky candy, popcorn or raw carrots. In addition, parents must keep certain things away from small children and babies, like balloons, coins, marbles, small toy parts, pen or marker caps and batteries.

Remember that choking kills thousands of people each year, but fast action in helping someone who is choking can save a life.

Multiple Choice

1. A person who is choking...

    a) will be coughing a lot.
    b) will ask you for your help.
    c) is not able to talk.

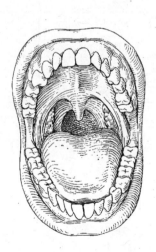

2. If you are doing a finger sweep, be careful not to...

    a) let the person bite your finger.
    b) push the food deeper into the throat.   c) sweep your finger about the person's mouth.

3. You can prevent choking by...

    a) cutting food into small pieces and chewing it very well.
    b) having your children always eat in a sitting position.
    c) keeping balloons, coins, marbles, small toy parts, pen or marker caps and batteries out of the hands of young children.
    d) all of the above.

Vocabulary Activity

Look at the words below that describe either dangerous foods for young children, dangerous household items or dangerous actions. Place them into one of the three columns. Then, try to think of two or three other things that could go into each column.

hot dogs, marbles, nuts, not chewing food thoroughly, pen or marker caps, large pieces of meat or cheese, eating food while laying down, batteries, whole grapes, eating food while walking around, hard or sticky candy, small toy parts, popcorn, raw carrots, balloons, coins, not cutting food into small pieces

Dangerous Foods	Dangerous Household Items	Dangerous Actions

911

911 is a telephone number. In most of North America the numbers 911 (nine one one) can save your life. Dial 911 if you have a serious problem. 911 will contact the fire department, the police, and an ambulance. If it is not an emergency, do not use 911. You do not have to put money in pay phones to call 911.

The people who answer 911 calls are called dispatchers. Dispatchers can help you in many ways. They can tell you what to do until help arrives and they can tell you when the help will come. Try to stay calm and answer the dispatcher's questions. If you can not talk because you are sick or you are unable to talk for some other reason, just dial 911 and wait. The dispatcher may be able to find you by tracing the call. Here is a typical 911 call:

Dispatcher: 911. What is your emergency?
Caller: There is a fire.
Dispatcher: What is the location of the fire?
Caller: It is at 110 Main Street.
Dispatcher: Thank you. Help is on the way. Please stay on the line.

911 is a telephone number that could save your life.

Multiple Choice

1. Which of the following is NOT a good reason to place a 911 call?

   a) A fire.
   b) Loud music.
   c) A car accident.
   d) A gun shot.

2. If you cannot speak for some reason you should...

   a) hang up.
   b) not call.
   c) stay on the line.

3. The 911 dispatcher will...

   a) contact the fire department.
   b) alert the police.
   c) dispatch an ambulance.
   d) all of the above.

Complete the Conversation

Dispatcher: 911 what is your emergency?

You: My friend _____.

Dispatcher: _____ address?

You: _____.

Dispatcher: I have alerted the _____. Help is _____

_____. Please stay _____.

Noun or Verb?

Many words in English can be either a noun (a person, place, or thing) or a verb (an action). The only way to decide is to look at the sentence:

People ANSWER 911 calls.   ANSWER is a VERB
Your ANSWER is correct.   ANSWER is a NOUN

Decide whether each ALL CAPITALS word below is a noun or a verb:

1. Here is a typical CALL.   NOUN   VERB

2. CALL the police! There is an accident.   NOUN   VERB

3. Dispatchers can HELP you in many ways.   NOUN   VERB

4. They will tell you when HELP will arrive.   NOUN   VERB

Earthquakes

An earthquake is a sudden shaking of the Earth that is caused by the breaking and shifting of rock under the Earth's surface. Most earthquakes in North America happen west of the Rocky Mountains, although some strong earthquakes have occurred in the central of the United States. Most of the strongest earthquakes in North America occur in Alaska, although it is possible to have an earthquake in any state or province on this continent.

An earthquake almost never kills anyone directly. Most deaths that occur during an earthquake will come from falling objects or from a building or bridge that collapses. An earthquake is one of the most powerful things on earth. A strong earthquake has energy that
is 10,000 times greater than the first atomic bomb. Earthquakes have made rivers change their path and have created huge tidal waves. Thousands of people have died as a result of earthquakes and one of the most famous earthquakes--the 1906 San Francisco earthquake and fire--destroyed most of that city.

The most dangerous places to be during earthquakes are just outside of buildings, by the exits or by the exterior walls. Most people who are injured in earthquakes are hurt by flying glass, falling objects and by walls that collapse. In the 1933 Long Beach, California earthquake, many people died because they ran outside and were struck by falling objects. The best way to be safe in an earthquake is to get under a heavy desk or table. The good news is that while over 50,000 earthquakes happen each

Multiple Choice

1. The famous 1906 San Francisco earthquake and fire...

   a) killed thousands of people.
   b) created a huge tidal wave.
   c) destroyed most of the city.

2. Most earthquakes in North America happen...

   a) west of the Rocky Mountains.
   b) in Alaska.
   c) in the central of the United States.

3. The safest place to be in an earthquake is...

   a) just outside a building.
   b) under a heavy desk.
   c) in Long Beach.

True Or False?

Put a T in the space provided if the statement about earthquakes is TRUE or an F if the statement is FALSE.

Earthquakes...

_____   1. have made rivers change their path and have created huge tidal waves.

_____   2. have killed thousands of people and once destroyed most of San Francisco.

_____   3. have energy that is 1,000 times greater than the first atomic bomb.

_____   4. happen mostly east of the Rocky Mountains in North America.

_____   5. cause breaking and shifting of rock deep below the Earth's surface.

Discussion Questions

1. The reading says that earthquakes are one of the most powerful and dangerous things on earth. Have you ever been in one? If so, what was it like? If not, what do you imagine it would be like?

2. Which of the following frightens you the most: an earthquake, a tornado, a fire or a dark street late at night? Why?

Electrical Fires

Electrical fires are fires that are caused by electricity. Electrical fires may start in old homes or old buildings. An electrician should check the electrical wires regularly and change any wires that become old and worn out. Electrical appliances, such as toasters, irons, microwave ovens, should also be checked on a regular basis. Electrical cords should never be under carpets or rugs because the cords could become worn and set the carpet or rug on fire.

Another common way electrical fires occur is when electrical outlets are overloaded. Electrical outlets are overloaded when too many appliances are plugged into one electrical socket. The socket receives too much electricity and becomes hot and may cause a fire. Overloading sockets can be especially dangerous when the socket is under a window that has drapes or curtains. The drapes or curtains can catch fire easily and quickly, and the fire can then spread throughout the house or building.

It is important to remember that electrical fires should never be put out with water. Water can make the situation much worse. A liquefied gas extinguisher, which contains either carbon dioxide or a gas called Halon, should always be used. There is also a dry chemical extinguisher that can be used to put out electrical fires.

Although electrical fires can be very dangerous, with a little common sense, they can be easily avoided.

Multiple Choice

1. Electrical fires may start in (check two of the following)...

   a) old homes.
   b) Old Faithful.
   c) old buildings.

2. Which of the following is not a cause of an electrical fire?

   a) Electrical appliances, such as toasters and irons, that have worn out cords.
   b) Overloading electrical sockets.
   c) Downloading electronic mail (e-mail).

3. What kind of fire extinguisher should be used in an electrical fire?

   a) A water extinguisher.
   b) A liquefied gas extinguisher.
   c) A foam extinguisher.

Vocabulary

Unscramble the words of appliances that could cause electrical fires.

1. RINO _____

2. ORESTAT _____

3. CROWMAVEI _____

Summarizing Information

Choose the best summary for each paragraph. Put summary letters in the correct spaces. Of the six (6) summaries, only four (4) can be used.

Paragraph 1 talks about _____

Paragraph 2 talks about _____

Paragraph 3 talks about _____

Paragraph 4 talks about _____

a) Why you should not buy old homes or used appliances.

b) There are several ways to put out electrical fires.

c) How old wires and appliances can start electrical fires.

d) The best ways to put out electrical fires.

e) By using common sense electrical fires can be avoided.

f) Electrical sockets and how these can start electrical fires.

Discussion Question

Do you think electrical fires are more common now than they were thirty years ago? Why or why not?

Smoke Alarms

Thousands of people die in fires every year. Most of these deaths happen in private homes. A house can be destroyed in minutes and fires often happen when people are asleep. The best way to survive a fire is to leave as quickly as possible. To do that, people need to know about a fire as soon as possible. Smoke alarms, also called smoke detectors, are a simple and cheap way to save your life. For a smoke alarm to be effective, it needs to be situated in the proper place, and they need to function properly.

It is difficult to understand why someone would not have a working smoke alarm in his or her home. They can cost as little as $10 and they are easy to install. In 1995, over 90% of homes in the United States had smoke alarms. But a survey found that over 16 million people had smoke alarms that did not work! Smoke alarms need batteries, and they also need to be cleaned. It is a good idea to check a smoke alarm at least once a month to make sure that it works. You should also change the battery at least once a year. Some smoke alarms beep suddenly when the battery is weak. A smoke alarm should last about 10 years. After that time, it is a good idea to buy another one.

In addition, smoke alarms need to be put in the best places. Put a smoke alarm in every bedroom and hallway. It is also a good idea to put one in the basement because many fires start there. Put the smoke alarm on the ceiling or high up on a wall because smoke will rise.

So, there are no more excuses! When you go home tonight, put in a smoke alarm if you do not have one. If you already have an alarm, test it.

Multiple Choice

1. A family has a smoke alarm that does not work. They probably need to...

   a) ignore it.
   b) check the battery.
   c) replace it.
   c) a & b.
   d) b & c.

2. A smoke alarm should cost around...

   a) $1,000.   b) $1.   c) $10.   d) $100.

3. Put a smoke alarm on...

   a) the floor.   b) the ceiling.   c) a bed.   d) a stove.

Sentence Completions

Conplete each sentence below.

1. Sixteen million people with smoke alarms _____.

2. A fire can destroy a house _____.

3. Many people die in a fire because _____.

4. You should put a smoke alarm in every _____ and _____.

Homphones

Homophones or homonyms are words that sound the same, but are spelled differently and have different meanings. Here is a list of common homophones:

Here/hear	weak/week	Buy/by
Two/to/too	one/won	Be/bee
I/eye	there/their	right/write
No/know	way/weigh	

It is very easy to confuse these words when you write them. Find the mistake in each of the sentences below and write the words correctly in the spaces provided.

1. Thousands of people dye in fires every year.   _____

2. People need to no about a fire as soon as possible.   _____

3. They are easy too install.   _____

4. Some smoke alarms beep suddenly when the battery is week.   _____

5. It is also a good idea to put won in the basement.   _____

22

First Aid Kits

First aid kits are important to have around your home or where you work. They have common medicines and supplies that you can use to help yourself or someone else. People often use first aid for cleaning and covering cuts and for headaches or other minor pain. If you have a few supplies on hand, you should be able to treat these problems easily. If you want, you can buy a first aid kit at most drug stores. Or, if you prefer, you can buy first aid items individually.

When someone has a cut, try to stop any bleeding that occurs. You should be able to do this by applying pressure to the cut using gauze or a clean cloth. After the bleeding stops, clean the wound with water or another solution like hydrogen peroxide. Your first aid kit should also have surgical tape and several different sizes of adhesive bandages to help you cover the cut. Remember that if the person continues to bleed or bleeds more after 5 minutes of pressure, you should call an ambulance or take the person to the hospital.

Another common problem is a headache or other pain, so your first aid kit should have aspirin and other pain relievers. Read the directions on the bottle to know how many tablets to take and to know how often you should take them. You should also take note of when you take the pill(s) so you know when to take the next one(s). After taking the medicine most people should feel better in 4-6 hours. It is also a good idea to have a thermometer to find out if the person has a fever. A normal temperature is 98.6 degrees F or 37 degrees C. If someone has frequent pain or fever, you should encourage him or her to visit a doctor.

Hopefully you will never have to use your first aid kit, but you will definitely feel better knowing that you can help yourself or someone else in a minor emergency.

Multiple Choice

1. We should use first aid kits to...

    a) replace a doctor.
    b) treat minor problems.
    c) be fashionable.

2. You should take a person who is bleeding to a hospital when the bleeding...

    a) becomes worse or does not stop. b) just begins. c) stops.

3. To stop bleeding you should...

    a) do nothing. b) take an aspirin. c) use gauze to apply pressure.

4. If you have a headache and want to take an aspirin you should first...

    a) read the directions. b) notice what time you took it. c) both of these.

Matching

Match each first aid supply listed below on the left with how it is used.

1. gauze   a. to relieve a minor pain

2. aspirin   b. to clean a wound

3. surgical tape   c. to cover a wound

4. thermometer   d. to hold gauze over a wound

5. hydrogen peroxide   e. to measure a person's temperature

Misspelled Words

Every word in the list below is spelled incorrectly. Find the correct spelling in the reading.

1. comon   _____

2. suplies   _____

3. individualy _____

4. bleding   _____

5. aplying   _____

6. diferent   _____

7. botle   _____

8. hopefuly   _____

What did you have to do to each word to correct it? _____

Fainting And Fever

Fainting is a result of not enough blood reaching the brain. When a person faints usually the person loses consciousness for only a short time. This loss of consciousness may have no medical importance or it can be a sign of a serious illness. If you feel faint, you should either lie down or sit down and put your head between your knees. If a person who has fainted falls to the floor, you should position the person on his or her back. Check the person's pulse and if breathing and heartbeat have stopped, you should begin Cardiopulmonary Resuscitation (CPR). To get blood back into the brain, you should put the person's feet higher than his or her head. Generally, the person will regain consciousness quickly.

Fever is a reaction of the body to an infection. Normally, our temperature does not go higher than 99 degrees Fahrenheit (98.6 degrees, which is the generally accepted normal temperature, is actually only a general guide). If your temperature reaches 103 degrees Fahrenheit, it is considered very serious and you need to see a doctor immediately. If a temperature of 101 degrees Fahrenheit lasts for over three days, you should also go to a doctor. You also should seek medical attention if in addition to a fever you have a bad headache, a stiff neck, a swollen throat or mental confusion. Aspirin or acetaminophen will help to bring down the temperature. A baby younger than three months with a fever should always be brought to a doctor.

Although fainting and fever may not be a sign of a serious medical condition, you should never ignore them.

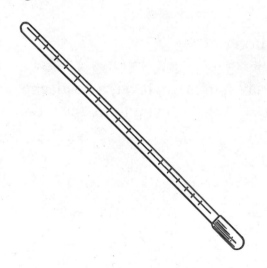

Multiple Choice

1. When a person faints, he or she usually loses consciousness for...

    a) several days.
    b) eight hours.
    c) a few moments.

2. To get blood back to the brain of the person who has fainted, you should...

    a) lie the person down and raise his or her legs.
    b) begin Cardiopulmonary Resuscitation (CPR).
    c) check the person's breathing and pulse.

3. A person should see a doctor if he or she has a fever...

    a) that is over 103 degrees Fahrenheit.
    b) that is over 101 degrees Fahrenheit and lasts for three days or more.
    c) and a bad headache or stiff neck.   d) all of the above.   e) none of the above.

Vocabulary

Below are groups of four (4) words. Three (3) of the words have something in common.
One (1) word in each group does not belong. Circle the word that does not belong.

1. head   knees   breathing   brain

2. fever   headache   swelling   body

3. sometimes   normally   usually   generally

4. position   reaction   put   place

You Are The Doctor

1. Make a list of symptoms of some illnesses, like a cold, the flu, the measles and malaria.

2. Make a list of five (5) situations that would be considered minor medical emergencies.

3. Make a list of five (5) situations that would be considered major medical emergencies.

Definition

We say fainting, a fever, a headache, a stiff neck or a swollen throat can be symptoms of an illness. What do you think the word symptom means?

Car Passenger Safety

Many people die in car accidents every year. There are some very simple ways to be safer in an automobile. First, adults should wear a seat belt. Most injuries happen when in a crash a passenger is thrown against a part of the car. A seat belt can hold an adult against the seat. To be effective, a seatbelt must be worn properly. Pregnant women should be especially careful about how to adjust the seatbelt. If you have any questions, ask a police officer or a medical professional to show you.

Second, babies and young children should have special seats. If you cannot afford to buy a child's seat, many organizations will give you one. Call your local police station for help. If you put the seat in the front, be sure to disable the air bag.

Third, avoid distracting the driver. An accident often happens when a driver looks away from the road. Do not make a loud noise or grab the driver because the driver needs to pay attention to driving. Make sure that you keep your arms inside the car when it is moving and that the car is completely stopped when you get in or out of the car. Also, do not touch the steering wheel or brake if you are not the driver.

Finally, be sure that the driver is capable to drive. If you see that a driver is intoxicated, do not get in the car. Attempt to get the keys and to talk the drunk person out of driving. Always remember, you are much safer walking or finding another way to travel than you are by riding with a drunk driver.

Being a passenger in a car can be safer if you follow these few simple steps.

Multiple Choice

1. An adult should wear a seat belt...

   a) occasionally.
   b) properly.
   c) only when there are children present.

2. The best place for young children is...

   a) in a special seat.
   b) in the driver's lap.
   c) where they want to be.

3. When a car is moving the driver's attention should be on...

   a) the passengers.   b) the road.   c) tuning the radio.

Find the Opposite

In the article on car passenger safety, find words with the opposite meanings of the words below.

1. Live   ____ i ____

2. Difficult   ____ ____ ____ ____ ____ e

3. Back   ____ r ____ ____ ____

4. Sober   ____ ____ ____ ____ k

5. Soft   ____ ____ ____ d

Find the Mistakes

There is a mistake in each sentence below. Find the mistake and re-write the sentence.

1. Small children should wear seat belts.

_____

2. Adults should have special seats.

_____

3. It is safer to ride with a driver that is drunk than it is to walk.

_____

Fun In The Sun

Summertime means family vacations, ocean beaches, lake swims and fun in the sun! Make sure your summer fun is also safe fun. Although the summer sun brings smiles to many faces, we must be careful of illnesses that are caused by the sun and the heat that accompanies it. One example of an illness that is principally caused by the sun is skin cancer. To avoid skin cancer try to stay out of the sun during the middle of the day and always try to use a sunscreen when you will be in direct sunlight.

Another illness caused by hot summer temperatures is heat stroke. Heat strokes can kill! Heat strokes happen when the body's system of controlling its temperature stops working. If the body's temperature is not cooled quickly, the person may die. If a person has hot, red and dry skin, difficulty breathing and problems staying awake, he or she may have heat stroke. Quickly try to cool the body with wet towels or by fanning. If you have ice, put it on the person's wrists, ankles, neck and in his or her armpits. Call 911 immediately.

One way to avoid illness caused by being out in the sun for long periods is to drink lots of water. Also, try not to drink alcohol or drinks with caffeine in them because those drinks can interfere with the body's ability to regulate temperature. It is also a good idea to protect your eyes. Sunglasses are like sunscreen for your eyes. They shield your eyes from harmful ultraviolet (UV) rays. Choose a pair of sunglasses which take out 90 percent of the UV sunlight.

Have fun in the sun this summer, but take care to not let the sun spoil your day!

Multiple Choice

1. An example of an illness caused by heat is...

   a) the flu.   b) skin cancer.
   c) heat stroke.   d) b and c.
   e) all of the above.

2. If a person has a heat stroke, he or she may have...

   a) hot, red and dry skin.   b) problems breathing.   c) difficulty staying awake.
   d) a and b.   e) all of the above.

3. If you are staying out in the sun for a long time, you should NOT...

   a) use sunscreen.   b) drink a lot of water.   c) drink alcohol or coffee.

Matching

Match the illness to what you can do to help or stop it from happening.

    1. skin cancer

    2. heat stroke

    3. eye problems

a) Quickly try to cool the body with wet towels or by fanning. If you have ice, put it on the person's wrists, ankles, neck and in his or her armpits. Call 911 for medical help immediately.

b) Choose a pair of sunglasses which take out 90 percent of the UV sunlight

c) Stay out of the sun during the middle of the day and always try to use a sunscreen.

Going To The Beach

Make a list of five or six things that you can take to the beach with you to protect you from the sun and heat.

1. _____

2. _____

3. _____

4. _____

5. _____

6. _____

Communicable Diseases

If you have ever had the flu, or an earache, you have had a communicable disease. Of course, there are other serious communicable diseases that can be deadly. Communicable diseases are diseases that can be transferred from one person to another. There are many other diseases that are not contagious. Communicable diseases come from viruses and bacteria. There are some easy things that can be done to lower the risk of catching a communicable disease. Simply put, you should handle food properly, use medicines correctly, and be careful around animals.

Most viruses and bacteria can be killed with soap, water, and a disinfectant. Do an extra good job of cleaning around places where you cook and eat. Many viruses and bacteria, for example, grow in uncooked meat. It is better to keep meats in the refrigerator until you are ready to cook it or eat it. Today, many raw meats come with safe handling instructions written on the label. Follow these directions. Of course, you should wash your hands often.

You should always be careful about how to use medicines to treat communicable diseases. Since communicable diseases can come from either a virus or bacteria, you need to use the correct medicine to treat it. For example, if you have a communicable disease that is from a virus, an antibiotic may make you sicker instead of helping you. It is always best to go to a doctor if your symptoms do not improve quickly.

Being careful around animals can also reduce your risk of getting sick. If you have a pet, make sure that it stays healthy. Many viruses and bacteria can travel from pets to humans. When you keep your pet healthy, you are also helping yourself. Also, be very careful about handling wild animals because they may carry more bacteria and viruses than pets do.

These easy things can reduce your chances of catching a communicable disease. Remember to wash your hands carefully, keep your pets healthy, and take the correct medicines when you feel ill.

Multiple Choice

1. To prevent communicable diseases you should...

   a) be clean.   b) use medicines correctly.
   c) be careful with animals. d) all of these.

2. Which of the following is NOT a good idea...

   a) taking an antibiotic without seeing a doctor.
   b) washing your hands often.
   c) keeping the kitchen clean.

3. Having a healthy pet helps you because...

   a) you will not get the flu. b) a disease may come from your pet to you.   c) it is cheaper.

Error Correction

Each of the sentences below contains one (1) mistake. Find the mistake and rewrite the sentence.

1. Washing your hands before you eat is unhealthy.

_____.

2. It is good for viruses and bacteria to be in your food.

_____.

3. Antibiotics are used to treat viral illnesses.

_____.

4. Sick pets are a benefit to their owners.

_____.

Building Words

Combine 1 half of a word from column A and 1 half from column B. All of these words come from the article.

A		B
1.	comunic	eases
2.	dis	able
3.	anti	cooked
4.	care	biotic
5.	un	ful

1. _____

2. _____

3. _____

4. _____

5. _____

Halloween Safety

Halloween is a night of witches, ghosts, super-heroes and cartoon characters. Here are some ideas to help make Halloween night fun and safe. Before going out trick and treating, parents and children should plan the route that the children will take. Parents and young children should go out together. The child's costume should be made from material that will not catch fire and there should be reflective markings or reflective tape on it. Be sure the costume is not so long that the child will trip and fall over it. Children must see properly out of a mask.

Young trick-or-treaters should carry flashlights with them and older kids should wear watches. Children should only go to houses that are lit and never go inside of a house. If the children are a little older and prefer to go trick-or-treating without their parents, they should make plans to go with friends and also carry a few quarters along with them or bring a cell phone so that they can call home. Children should never eat candy before returning home.

Once the children return home, the candy should be inspected carefully before it is eaten. Look for holes in the candy wrapper or a wrapper that has already been opened. Nowadays, some parents choose to give treats other than candy, for example rub-on tattoos, small coloring books or stickers. Instead of trick-or-treating, many modern parents prefer to give parties where children can dress up and play with friends while enjoying games, pumpkin cookies and other treats.

Halloween is meant to be fun and filled with surprise, but do not forget some common sense rules that will make it safe for all.

Multiple Choice

1. Before going out trick-or-treating, parents and children should...

   a) plan where children will trick-or-treat.
   b) put reflective markings or reflective tape on the costume.
   c) make sure the child's costume is not too long.
   d) all of the above.

2. Children should begin to eat their candy...

   a) as soon as they get it.   b) when they get hungry.
   c) only after they have returned home and inspected it carefully with a parent.

3. Instead of trick-or-treating, many modern parents...

   a) give Halloween parties.   b) tell their children to forget about Halloween.
   c) give their children rub-on tattoos and small coloring books.

Jack-O'-Lanterns

Circle the word in the parenthesis that best fits in the sentence.

1. Jack-o'-lanterns are (pumpkins/watermelons) with a funny or scary face cut in them.

2. Most jack-o'-lanterns have a (crayon/candle) inside of them.

3. In Irish legend, jack-o'-lanterns where named after a man called (Jack/Albert) who was not allowed to enter either heaven or (a foreign country/hell) and as a result, had to walk the earth forever with his (dog/lantern).

Discussion Questions

1. Halloween probably began to be celebrated over 2,000 years ago by the Celts in what is now England. It was a celebration of their New Year which began on November 1st. These days Halloween is celebrated in many countries throughout the world. Why do you think it has become such a popular holiday?

2. Have you ever gone out on Halloween? What was your costume? What kind of candy did you collect?

3. Do you believe in ghosts? Do you know any ghost stories?

Avoiding Victimization

Anyone can be a victim of a crime. Sometimes, there is nothing you can do to stop a criminal. Most of the time, though, there are ways to avoid being a victim. Three easy things to remember to avoid being a victim of a crime are: knowing the area where you travel, to never travel alone, and ignoring anyone who tries to bother you.

It is always a good idea to know as much as you can about your surroundings. For example, if you know where the best-lit streets are, you should use them and avoid going through dark alleys and other more dangerous avenues. You should know where to find various kinds of help if you need it. Be able to find places like hospitals, fire and police stations, and stores that have more pedestrian and vehicle traffic.

Try to stay around other people. Also, if you go anywhere, it is a good practice to go with a friend. People who walk or drive by themselves are much easier to attack. It is smart to use streets that have a lot of people on them. Also, be very careful when you meet someone for the first time. It is a good practice to arrange a first time meeting in a public place instead of in a home or in a hotel room.

If someone tries to bother you, ignore that person and move away. Do not shout at the person or try to hit the person. It is wiser to stay calm and attempt to move to a safe area. Be sure to call the police, so they can investigate. If someone wants to steal your purse or wallet, it is safer to give it to the person and try to remember what he or she looks like. Nothing you carry is worth your life.

There is a difference between being safe and being afraid. If you have thought ahead, you do not have to be afraid.

MULTIPE CHOICE

1. It is safer to walk in a...

   a) dark alley.
   b) neighborhood you do not know.
   c) park at night.
   d) shopping center.

2. The safest place to meet someone for the first time is your...

   a) hotel room.   b) favorite restaurant.   c) car.   d) home.

3. If a criminal bothers you, you should...

   a) slap him.   b) move away and call the police.   c) argue with him.   d) call your friend.

Word Endings

Find a word for each definition below from the reading.

1. _____: a person who commits a crime

2. _____: areas that surround you

3. _____: a person who walks

Infinintives

Infinitives are often easy to find.   Most of the time, they have the word TO and a VERB.

For example:

There are ways TO AVOID being a victim.

Notice that there is always another verb in a sentence with an infinitive.

Circle five (5) examples of infinitives in the paragraph below.

Try to stay around other people. Also, if you go anywhere, it is a good practice to go with a friend with you. People who walk or drive by themselves are much easier to attack.   It is smart to use streets that have a lot of people on them. Also, be very careful when you meet someone for the first time.   It is a good practice to arrange a first time meeting in a public place instead of in a home or in a hotel room.

Christmastime Safety

Christmastime is a happy time for most people. People enjoy parties, decorating and being with friends and family; however, it is important not to forget safety during the holiday season. There are a few easy things we need to remember to avoid accidents. The first thing is to be very careful when using candles. Always keep candles away from material that can catch on fire, like curtains or holiday decorations. Never use candles on your Christmas tree. Also, remember to never leave children alone in a room with lit candles.

Christmas trees are the cause of hundreds of fires each year. Artificial trees are safer and cleaner than real trees. They are safer because they are made with nonflammable materials, and they are cleaner because they do not have so many falling needles. If you do buy a real tree, make sure you water it daily and place it away from sources of heat, like heat registers and fireplaces. Also, put the tree in a stand that will be strong enough to hold the tree up without falling over.

Many people have parties during the holidays. If you are giving a party, try not to use candles and use decorations that cannot catch fire. If your guests will smoke indoors, make sure there are plenty of ashtrays. If you are going to a party where alcohol will be served, it is a good idea to choose a "designated driver"; that is, someone who will not drink alcohol during the party. That person can drive his or her friends home.

Remember these safety tips and have a great holiday season!

Multiple Choice

1. Lit candles can be dangerous when...

   a) they are placed on trees.
   b) they are placed near curtains or holiday decorations.
   c) they are in rooms with children present, but no adults.
   d) all of the above.

2. If you are having a party and you know there will be smokers coming, you should...

   a) ask them to smoke in the bathroom.   b) have a lot of ashtrays for them.
   c) have the smokers choose a designated driver.

3. If you are planning to go to a party and to drink alcohol, a safe thing to do is to...

   a) bring a lot of ice.
   b) drive someone else's car.
   c) choose a designated driver.

Correct The Mistake

Find the mistakes in the following sentences and then rewrite the sentences.

1. Always use candles as decorations on Christmas trees.

_____.

2. Christmas trees cause hundreds of fires each month.

_____.

3. Real trees are safer and cleaner than artificial trees.

_____.

4. If you buy a real Christmas tree, you should water it at least once a week.

_____.

5. Make sure you place the tree in a sink that is strong enough to hold it.

_____.

Discussion Questions

1. Where do you think the term "designated driver" comes from? Why is it so important to have a designated driver?

2. In what ways does alcohol affect one's ability to drive? Do you know how many drinks it would take in your state or province to be considered legally drunk?

Drug And Vitamin Labels

There are hundreds of drugs and vitamins in stores. Some of them can help and some can cause serious harm. The best way to decide if a drug or vitamin is good for you is to ask a doctor or pharmacist. In addition, it is important to read the labels on the package. There are 3 major kinds of drugs and vitamins: prescription drugs, over the counter drugs, and vitamins.

You should only take a prescription drug if a doctor tells you to take it. Make sure that you understand when and how to take the drug. Also, make sure that you know what you may feel when you take it. Finally, make sure that you understand what to do if there is a serious reaction.

Almost anyone can buy over the counter drugs. Examples of over the counter drugs include aspirin and cold medicines. Be sure that you read the label on the bottle. If the package or bottle is open, do not buy it. Be sure that you understand how to take the medicine. You should know the name of the product, how much you need to take, and when to stop taking it. Also, most medicine has an expiration date. Do not take the medicine after the date on the package.

Finally, there are vitamins. The government is not as strict with vitamins as it is with drugs, so you need to read more carefully. Always understand how much of a vitamin you need to take and how it may react with other drugs or vitamins. If you are not sure, ask a doctor or pharmacist for help.

All of these chemicals can help you if you use them correctly. Remember that it is better to be safe than sorry.

Multiple Choice

1. Which of the following is NOT important to know about a drug or vitamin...

   a) how many people take it.
   b) the expiration date.
   c) how much to take.
   d) when to take it.

2. If you are not sure about which drug or vitamin to take you should...

   a) ask a doctor.   b) read the label.   c) ask a pharmacist. d) all of these.

3. A label will NOT tell you...

   a) the expiration date. b) how often to take it. c) your allergies.

Definitions

Write your own definition to each of the following:

1. Prescription drug: _____

2. Over the counter drug: _____

3. Expiration date: _____

Correct The Mistakes

Each sentence below has a mistake in it.   Find the mistake and rewrite the sentence.

1. The best way to decide if a drug or vitamin is good for you is to ask a friend.

_____.

2. Make sure that you ignore what side effects you could feel when you take a drug.

_____.

3. Do not take the medicine after the date on the receipt.

_____.

4. The government is more strict with vitamins than it is with drugs.

_____.

Myths About Seat Belts

A myth is a story or a belief that many people believe to be true, but it is actually untrue. We have all heard many myths regarding the use of seat belts. "Seat belts are for longer trips. You don't need them for short trips around town." "My uncle wasn't wearing a seat belt and he was saved when he was thrown from his car during an accident." "If I wear a seat belt, I might be trapped if my car catches on fire or goes under water." Let us take a closer look at the reasons why each of these statements are myths.

Myth #1 "Seat belts are for longer trips. You don't need them for short trips around town." The fact is that three out of four deaths from car accidents happen within 25 miles (40 kilometers) of home and four out of five accidents happen at speeds of less than 40 miles per hour (64 kilometers per hour). Statistics show that seat belts give you a 45% better chance of surviving if you are in a crash.

Myth #2 "My uncle wasn't wearing a seat belt and he was saved when he was thrown from his car during an accident." Generally, passengers thrown from a car are thrown through the windshield and they are injured as a result. The fact is you are 25 times more likely to die if you are thrown from your car, rather than being belted in.

Myth #3 "If you wear a seat belt, you might be trapped if your car catches on fire or goes under water" The fact is that accidents that involve fire or water are rare. But even if you are in an accident that has fire or water, you will still be safer if you are wearing a seat belt! If you are not wearing a seat belt before the crash, you could hit your head during the accident and become unconscious and then be trapped, or else you could be thrown from the car (see Myth #2).

Do not believe these myths about seat belts. Seat belts not only make sense, they save lives!

Multiple Choice

1. Most accidents happen within...

   a) 25 miles (40 kilometers) of home.
   b) 40 miles (64 kilometers) of home.
   c) 125 miles (202 kilometers) of home.

2. Accidents that involve fire or water...

   a) are very common.   b) frequently occur.
   c) are not very common.

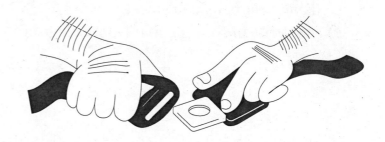

3. If you are thrown from a car in an accident, you will probably go...

   a) through the side door. b) through the front window. c) through the back window.

More Myths

Here are some other myths about wearing seat belts. Do you know or can you guess why they are myths?

1. "You do not need a seat belt when you have air bags."

2. "It takes too much time and it is too much trouble to put on my seat belt."

3. "Seat belts are uncomfortable and I feel a loss of freedom when I wear them."

Discussion Questions

1. Do you wear your seat belt? Why? Why not? Do you know anyone who does not wear their seat belt?

2. Do you believe any of the so-called myths about seatbelts?

3. Can you think of anything else, whether about seat belts or anything else, that might be considered a myth?

The Main Idea

The main idea of this article is that...

    a) nowadays, all cars have seat belts.
    b) using seat belts can save lives.
    c) seat belts prevent people from being thrown from their cars during accidents.

Safety For Disabled People

Disabled people are people with special needs. Some special needs people may use a wheelchair. Others may be deaf or blind. Also remember that many other people have disabilities that are more difficult to recognize.

It is important to know about assigned places for disabled people and to understand how these help them to be safe. Most public buildings have special parking places for people in wheelchairs and special ramps to make the buildings accessible. Parking places for special needs people are often painted blue with a drawing of a wheelchair. This symbol means that a parking place can only be used by someone with a disability. For these people, a parking place that is a long distance from a building or a building without a ramp can make a trip dangerous or impossible.

On a bus or train or subway seats with the same drawing of a wheelchair are reserved for people who may not be able to stand. If unauthorized people use these seats or the parking places mentioned above, they may be required to pay a large fine.

Disabled people may need more time to perform certain actions. Be especially careful when you are driving and see a disabled person crossing a street. They will probably need more time to cross. Also understand that they may need more time to climb stairs or do other actions like going in or out of buildings or vehicles. Try to give them more time and space to move. If you see a disabled person who struggles to do something, it is okay to offer to help but listen to their directions. Many times, the best way to help is not obvious.

Disabled people rarely want your pity. Instead, they probably only ask for and need your respect.

Multiple Choice

1. Special parking places for disabled people...

   a) are difficult to recognize.
   b) increase their safety.
   c) make parking lots more dangerous.

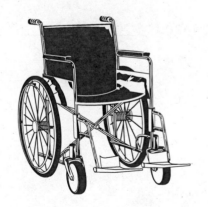

2. If you are an able-bodied person looking for a parking place and see a space painted blue with a drawing of a wheelchair, you should...

   a) park there any way.   b) pretend that you are disabled. c) find another place.

3. Disabled people probably mostly want...

   a) to be left alone.   b) your respect.   c) your pity.

Finding Examples

Think of an example for each of the following:

1. A task that may take longer for a disabled person.

_____

2. Things that have been done to aid special needs people.

_____

Adjectives.

Remember that adjectives are words that modify or explain nouns. Unscramble the letter below to form ten (10) adjectives. All of them come from the reading.

1. dleadbsi	_____	2. seialpc	_____
3. gearl	_____	4. unthrzdauoie	_____
5. cacslbesie	_____	6. licpbu	_____
7. searounged	_____	8. posesilimb	_____
9. lfrcaeu	_____	10. ouivobs	_____

Playgrounds

People of all ages love playgrounds. However, before 1900, there were few public playgrounds. Back then children had to play on their lawns, in vacant lots and in the street. The movement for public playgrounds was started shortly before 1900 by a New York City newpaperman, Jacob Riis, and then it spread throughout North America. Riis was responsible for creating the first public playground in New York City. Today, public playgrounds are found in every city and town. While playgrounds are much safer places than vacant lots or city streets used to be, they are not without danger.

Over 200,000 children are hurt each year as a result of playground accidents--that is one playground accident every two-and-a-half minutes. Most of these accidents, about 70%, happen when children fall from playground equipment. The most common injuries are fractures (39%), cuts (22%), bruises (20%), strains/sprains (11%). There are several ways to prevent these accidents. Adult supervision is important. In addition, the ground beneath the playground equipment must be soft; wood chips or fine sand can be used to make it soft. Also, playground equipment must be inspected regularly. Finally, children should be told to never walk too close to a moving swing because they can be hit unintentionally by another child who is swinging.

Remember these tips and keep your playground safe for everybody!

Multiple Choice

1. The movement for public playgrounds began...

    a) a little before 1900.
    b) a little after 1900.
    c) in 1900.

2. The majority of playground accidents are from...

    a) children fighting each other.
    b) falls from playground equipment.
    c) getting hit by a moving swing.

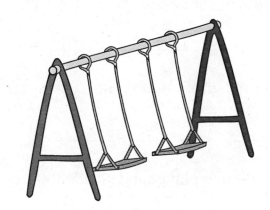

3. What kind of surface should not be under playground equipment?

    a. Sand.
    b. Wood chips.
    c. Concrete.

Match The Sentence Parts

_____   1. Before 1900, children living in large cities played mostly...

_____   2. Jacob Riis was responsible for...

_____   3. Today, public playgrounds can be found...

_____   4. While playgrounds are much safer places than vacant lots or city streets...

a. they are not without danger.
b. in almost every city and town in North America.
c. on their lawns, in vacant lots and in the street.
d. creating the first public playground New York City.

Statistics

The article on playgrounds provides many statistics. Complete the following by giving the correct statistic.

1. The percentage of playground accidents that involve falls.

_____

2. The number of children hurt each year in playground accidents.

_____

3. How often a playgound accident occurs.

_____

4. The percentage of playground accidents that are strains or sprains.

_____

Discussion Questions

Which do you think is more important for a community, a public playground or a public library? Imagine that your community has some extra money to spend, but cannot afford to build both a playground and a library. Which one would you like to see built and why?

School Safety

Schools should be safe places, and they are most of the time. However, students and parents can do a few things to make schools safer. Most importantly, both students and parents need to be more aware. Parents need to be observant of their children's behavior and students should understand more about their school's environment.

First of all, parents should be involved in their children's school. Children will always need their parents to take an interest in their lives and be there to give advice. If parents notice a sudden change in their child's behavior, they should contact the school to find out if the school staff has noticed this change in behavior and if his or her teachers know what is causing this change. Obviously, the best way to find out about your own children is to talk to them! Generally, the more a parent knows about their children and the school, the safer the children will be.

Students also need to be more responsible for their own safety at school. They should share their class schedule with a few friends and their parents. They should also try to avoid being at the school alone, especially late at night. Finally, they need to be more in control of their own actions, especially at social functions. When students have more knowledge about their own environment and that of their friends, they can prevent many safety problems.

Everyone is responsible for school safety. Most educators take their students' safety very seriously. However, they need parents and students to be responsible as well. When all of these groups work together, a school can be one of the safest and most productive places.

Multiple Choice

1. Parents and students have _____ about school safety.

    a) no responsibility
    b) all of the responsibility
    c) shared responsibility

2. Parents should...

a) be aware of their child's behavior.   b) ignore their child's behavior.   c) all of these.

3. To be safer, students should...

a) make sure friends and family know their routine.   b) be more responsible.   c) all of these.

Details

Look at the following examples. Fill in the blanks.

1. Jack's father listens carefully to his children and helps them with their homework.

   This is an example of _____

2. Jane tells her mother that she will be home late because she has soccer practice.

   This is an example of _____

The Apostrophe

The English language uses the apostrophe in 2 ways:

To show possession: Craig's desk is messy.
                        The students' homework was very good.

(Notice in the word students' that when the noun is plural, the apostrophe goes after the S.)

or

To take the place of letters in a contraction: Don't be afraid to talk to your children
                                        You can't come to the dance?

(Don't is the contraction for do not. Can't is the contraction for cannot.)

Rewrite each of the following sentences moving the apostrophe showing possession to its correct position.

1. If parents' notice a sudden change in their childs behavior, they should investigate.

_____

2. Parents need to be observant of their childrens behavior's.

_____

3. Parents' should be involved in their childrens school.

_____

Protecting Your Ears

You have maybe heard the expression, "I'm all ears." Of course, in reality, we have only two and those two ears can never be replaced. One thing we must do is protect our ears from prolonged exposure to loud noises, for example noisy machines or loud music. Having to listen to loud noises over a period of time can lead to hearing loss. To protect ourselves we must reduce the time we spend hearing those loud noises. In addition, we should always wear hearing protection when we are around noisy machines, including power tools, motorcycles, leaf blowers and lawn mowers.

Children sometimes get things stuck in their ears. Sometimes the object will come loose if you tip the head and shake it. If you can clearly see the object, try carefully removing it with a pair of tweezers.

However, if the object does not pull out easily or does not fall out after you gently shake your head, you need to see a doctor to have it removed. The most common reason for an ear injury to occur is when people accidentally hurt the ear while trying to remove an object. Also, insects and bugs can get stuck in your ear. Try washing an insect out of the ear with warm water.

Keep in mind there is an old saying that you should not put anything smaller than your elbow in your ear. Many old sayings are not true, but this one is. Cotton swabs and other objects people use to scratch or clean their ears can easily hurt them.

Be careful. Remember, like your eyes, you only have one pair of ears. Protect them!

Multiple Choice

1. One way to protect our hearing is to...

   a) use cotton swabs to keep your ears clean.
   b) spend less time in places where there are loud noises.
   c) use power tools, like electric drills and saws.

2. If you get an object stuck in your ear and it does not easily come out, you should...

   a) try using your little finger to remove it.
   b) use a pair of tweezers to force it out.
   c) see a doctor to have it removed.

3. One way to remove an insect that gets stuck in your ear is by...

   a) washing it out with warm water.
   b) washing it out with hot water.
   c) using your elbow to gently take it out.

Vocabulary

Circle the correct answer.

1. We must pay special attention to our ears, because they can never be (repaired / replaced).

2. If you can clearly see the object, try carefully removing it with a pair of (tweezers / twisters).

3. Sometimes the object will come loose, if you (tip / slip) the head and shake it.

4. There is an old saying that you should not put anything smaller than your (ankle / elbow) in your ear.

5. Remember, like your eyes, you only have one (pear / pair) of ears.

Noisy Things

Make a list of ten (10) loud things to which prolonged exposure could damage your hearing.

1. _____   2. _____

3. _____   4. _____

5. _____   6. _____

7. _____   8. _____

9. _____   10. _____

Discussion Questions

1. In your opinion, which of your five senses (sight/smell/hearing/touch/taste) is the most important? Why?

2. Which is the second most important? Why?

3. Which sense do you think you would have the most trouble living without? Why?

Animal Bites

Animals will often bite when they are afraid or angry. An animal is also more likely to bite if it has just given birth or if it is injured. If an animal growls, hisses, or makes other menacing sounds, it is probably trying to warn you. It may also show its teeth, bend its ears back, and tighten its muscles. Do not try to touch an animal when it is agitated and do not make any loud noises or sudden movements. Slowly back away from the animal.

Most people are bitten by pets, mainly dogs and cats. Dogs bite more people but cat bites get infected more often. Bites from wild or stray animals are more dangerous because these animals may have rabies. Rabies is a disease that can kill animals and people. If an animal acts strangely, foams at the mouth or attacks for no reason, it may have rabies. If you think that a rabid animal has bitten someone, take that person to the hospital or a doctor immediately. Be prepared to describe the animal to the doctor. However, do not try to catch the animal.

Most bites that come from pets are not serious. If the bite is not deep, clean the wound with soap and water. Apply an antibiotic cream and cover it. If the bite is deep, stop any bleeding by applying pressure and go to a doctor. If you have not had a tetanus shot in the last 10 years, be sure to get one for any bite that breaks the skin.

Animals can be good friends. As with all friends, treat animals with respect.

Multiple Choice

1. An animal that is angry or afraid may...

    a) wag its tail.
    b) growl or hiss.
    c) lick your hand.

2. If you see an animal that is agitated, you should...

    a) shout at it.
    b) move away from it.
    c) pet it.

3. The most dangerous kind of bites are from...

    a) cats.   b) dogs.   c) pets.   d) wild animals.

Finding Details

Find two (2) details in the article for each main idea below.

1. If an animal appears to be angry or afraid you should not...

_____

_____

2. If an animal has rabies it may...

_____

_____

And, Or, & But

Words such as AND, OR, and BUT are conjunctions. We use these words to join ideas together.

We use AND to join ideas that are similar:

   Cats AND dogs are similar.

We use BUT to join ideas that are opposite:

   Dogs bite more people BUT cat bites are more dangerous.

We us OR to include only one idea in a group:

   Take that person to the hospital OR to a doctor immediately.

Each of the following sentences needs a conjunction. Decide which conjunction is needed and rewrite the sentence.

1. It may also show its teeth, bend its ears back, _____ tighten its muscles.

_____.

2. An animal is more likely to bite if it has just given birth _____ if it is injured.

_____.

3. I like dogs _____ I do not like cats.

_____.

Protecting Your Eyes

"An ounce of prevention is worth a pound of cure." That old saying was never more true than when talking about the safety of our eyes. Thousands of eye injuries occur each day. Experts believe over 90% of those accidents would have been prevented if the correct eyewear had been worn.

Because of good safety rules in the workplace, the home has become the place where eye injuries usually happen. Parents can protect not only their children but themselves too by following a few common sense rules. Parents should not buy toys that have sharp points or edges, nor should parents buy flying toys or toys that shoot plastic bullets. Of course, BB guns, bows and arrows, and darts are extremely dangerous. In addition, always use safety glasses when using dangerous power tools or handling chemicals and remember that bystanders are in almost equal danger as the people who are using the tools or handling the chemicals.

Proper eye protection should be used when playing sports. For baseball and hockey, helmets can be bought that have face shields and for basketball or racquet sports, safety goggles can be purchased. Make sure the face shield or the goggles are made of polycarbonate, a very strong material. It is also very important that the helmets fit properly: a poorly fitting helmet will not give maximum protection.

If you do happen to be hit in the eye. Do not rinse the eye with water, nor should you try to remove an object that is stuck in your eye. You may gently put a small cold cloth to the eye to reduce the pain and swelling, and then go immediately to see a doctor.

Remember, though, when we are talking about eyes, "An ounce of prevention is worth a pound of cure."

Multiple Choice

1. These days eye injuries are becoming more and more common...

   a) at work.
   b) at home.
   c) at the optometrist's office.

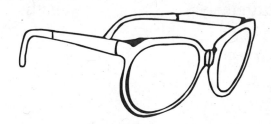

2. What should you do if you are hit in the eye...

   a) clean the eye with water.
   b) very gently put something cold to the eye to lessen swelling and pain.
   c) go to a doctor's office or hospital.   d) a and c.   e) b and c.

3. When buying a baseball or hockey helmet, make sure...

   a) it has a face shield. b) it is the right size.
   c) the face shield is made of polycarbonate material.   d) all of the above.

True Or False?

Here are some things people frequently say about our eyes. In a small group, talk about them and decide if they are true or false. Talk about the reasons why you believe they are true or false. Afterwards, look at the back of this book for the answers.

_____ 1. Eating carrots will make your eyesight better.

_____ 2. If you do not use your eye glasses, it will hurt your eyes even more.

_____ 3. An eye examination is only necessary if you are having problems seeing.

_____ 4. Reading in poor light can hurt your eyes. .

_____ 5. There is nothing you can do to save the loss of your eyesight.

Synonyms Or Antonyms?

Look at the two words. Decide if they are synonyms (words that have the same meaning) or antonyms (words that have the opposite meaning).

1. usually   rarely   synonym / antonym

2. maximum   most   synonym / antonym

3. remove   put   synonym / antonym

4. extremely   slightly   synonym / antonym

5. protect   safeguard   synonym / antonym

Fire Exits

A fire exit is a door or window that a person can use to leave a burning building. Similarly, a fire escape is an alternate staircase or passage that people can follow to safety. Most cities have very strict laws about fire exits. They can save your life if you know where they are and if they are properly maintained. There are 3 rules to remember about fire exits and fire escapes: 1) know where they are 2) know when to use them and 3) make sure that they can be used.

Sadly, most people die in fires in their own home. This seems strange because a person's home is the place they know better than any other. However, if a door is blocked or if a family panics, they often die before they can get out. A family should practice what to do if there is a fire. They should pretend that certain doors are blocked and learn how to open windows and other doors. It is a good idea to know where fire exits are in other buildings too. Most of the time, they will have a red sign that says EXIT or FIRE EXIT if it is a special exit to be used only during a fire.

People should know when to use a fire escape. If there is a fire, do not try to use an elevator. Use the stairs instead. Also, many people wait too long before leaving a building. A fire can destroy a room in less than 3 minutes. If you see a fire or hear a fire alarm, leave the area immediately and find the nearest exit. If a fire blocks an exit, find another one. Attempting to run through a fire should be your last choice, not your first.

Remember to never block a fire exit or block a door that leads to a fire exit. Keep these areas clean. People should be able to move through doors and stairways without falling over anything. Keep in mind that it can be difficult to see during a fire, so it is also a good idea to have stairways well lit. If you see a problem with a fire exit, fix it or tell the person who is responsible.

Fire exits are most efficient if you know about them before a fire.

Multiple Choice

1. Fires kill more people in...

   a) offices.
   b) hotels.
   c) stadiums.
   d) homes.

2. If a fire blocks an exit, you should...

   a) find another exit. b) wait for the fire to get smaller. c) run through the fire.

3. A fire exit should NEVER have...

   a) lights. b) a fire hose. c) a blocked door. d) a sign.

Opposites

In the reading, find the word with the opposite meaning of the following words.

1. entrance   ___ ___ ___ t

2. forget   ___ ___ ___ ___ ___ ___ ___ ___ r

3. normal   ___ ___ ___ ___ ___ ___ e

4. build   ___ ___ ___ ___ ___ ___ y

5. clear   ___ ___ ___ ___ k

Memory

Without looking back at the article, list the three (3) rules to remember about fire exits and fire escapes.

1. _____.

2. _____.

3. _____.

Poisoning

A poison is something that is dangerous to your life and health. Cleaning materials, for example, are often poisonous and certain medications, when not taken correctly, can also be poisonous. Most houses have some poisonous items in them; however, with a little thought and planning, most poisonings that occur in the home can be avoided.

If you think someone has swallowed a poison, you must take action quickly. First, look in the person's mouth and remove anything that is still in there. Next, look for the bottle or container of the thing that was swallowed. You will need this information for your next step, which is to call either a poison control center or 911. You will probably be asked the following questions: What was taken? When was it taken? How much was taken? How is the patient acting? You should tell the person from the poison control center or the 911 dispatcher who you are and your relationship with the patient, as well as the patient's age and weight.

You then must follow the poison center's directions. Remember that with some poisons, you will want the patient to vomit, but with other poisons--gasoline, cleaning materials and lighter fluids--you do not want the patient to vomit. If you are told to have the patient vomit, you could use a medicine called Ipecac syrup, which will make the patient throw up. If you do not have Ipecac syrup, you could gently touch the back of the patient's throat with your finger.

On the labels of most poisonous materials, there are instructions telling you what to do in case of poisoning. However, it is always best to telephone a poison control center and remember that prevention is the most important thing of all.

Multiple Choice

1. How can most poisonings in the home be avoided?

   a) By following the instructions of a poison control center.
   b) By giving the patient Ipecac syrup.
   c) With a little thought and planning.

2. What is one question that will be probably not be asked by the poison control center?

   a) What was taken?   b) How much was taken?   c) How tall is the patient?

3. The patient should never try to vomit if he or she has taken...

   a) lighter fluids.   b) cleaning materials.
   c) gasoline.   d) any of the above.

Match The Sentence Parts

_____   1. Most poisonings that happen in the home can be avoided...

_____   2. You must take action quickly...

_____   3. With some poisons, you want the patient to vomit, but with others...

_____   4. On the labels of most poisonous materials...

a. there are instructions telling you what to do in case of poisoning.
b. with a little thought and planning.
c. you do not want the patient to vomit.
d. if you think someone has swallowed a poison.

Summarizing Information

Choose the best summary for each paragraph. Put summary letters in the correct spaces. Of the six summaries (6), only four (4) can be used.

Paragraph 1 talks about _____

Paragraph 2 talks about _____

Paragraph 3 talks about _____

Paragraph 4 talks about _____

a) The fact that there are different methods for treating different poisons.

b) How to treat someone with Ipecac syrup.

c) Action to take when someone swallows poison.

d) Descriptions of some poisonous materials.

e) Prevention is the most important thing of all.

f) What a poison is.

Discussion Questions

Make a list of all materials and products in your house that you think could be poisonous. Where does your family keep them? Do you think these are safe places for the materials? Why or why not?

Pedestrian Safety

Over one million people die every year by simply walking along the street. If you follow some simple advice, you will be a safe pedestrian. Remember to ask yourself three questions to help you: When is it safe to walk? Where is it safe to walk? How is it safe to walk?

When is it safe to walk? The simple answer is when the driver and the pedestrian can see each other. Before you cross a street, be sure to look both ways and be sure that any driver can see you. Be aware that plants, snow, or other objects may block your or the driver's view. Try not to walk at these places and be especially careful if you have no other choice. Also, if you walk at night, it is best to have a flashlight with you and to wear bright or reflective clothing.

Where is it safe to walk? It is always safer to use a sidewalk or other areas for pedestrians. If there is no sidewalk, be sure to walk facing the traffic so you can see any cars coming. When you have to cross a street, do it at a traffic light or stop sign.

How is it safe to walk? Be aware of the traffic around you. Listen and watch attentively. Most accidents happen when pedestrians are not careful about where they are walking. If there is fog, rain or snow, remember that it will take a driver a longer time to see you, so leave even more space than normal. Also, understand that larger vehicles like trucks or buses need more distance to stop than a car.

In many places, walking is the easiest and safest way to travel. When we walk, though, we must remember that we have to share the street with vehicles.

Multiple Choice

1. Which is the best place to cross the street?

   a) At the "do not cross" sign.
   b) Over a snow pile.
   c) At a traffic light.

2. If you are walking where there is no sidewalk, walk...

   a) facing traffic. b) with your back to traffic. c) in the middle of the street.

3. When should you allow more time for a vehicle to stop?

a) When there is rain or snow. b) When the vehicle is a bus or truck. c) Both of these.

Imperatives

We use imperatives to give directions. They are verbs without a subject:

For example: Be sure to look both ways.

Find 3 imperatives in the reading above.

1. _____

2. _____

3. _____

Bad Advice

Each sentence below gives some bad advice advice. Rewrite each sentence so that it contains good advice.

1. You should walk away from the traffic. You will not be afraid that way.

_____.

2. At night, do not use a flashlight. A driver will believe you are another car.

_____.

3. Don't walk on the sidewalk because everyone else walks there. Be different!

_____.

Stress

Do you have frequent headaches? Do you smoke too much or sweat a lot? Do you feel tired all the time, but have trouble sleeping? Do you need to go to the bathroom frequently? Do you have trouble concentrating? Do you often have stomachaches or diarrhea? Have you gained or lost a great deal of weight lately? Do you have lower back pain, chest pain or neck pain? Have you felt dizzy lately? Do you have frequent nightmares?

If you answered yes to some of the questions above you may have stress. Stress is a reaction of your body to problems in your life. Driving in heavy traffic, being hurried, breaking up with a boy or girlfriend, losing a job or doing poorly at school are all possible causes of stress. In addition, the food we eat, the people around us and the things we do can also result in stress in our lives. If so many things can cause stress, how can we possibly avoid it?

There are several things we can do to lower stress. One thing is to play a sport or do some kind of physical activity, like swimming, tennis, bicycling, walking or yoga. Another thing you can do is to eat right. Always have a good breakfast and try to not have too much caffeine and sugar. Lastly, do not try to do too much. While working and studying are important, we need time to relax and enjoy life as well.

Remember the old saying: All work and no play make Jack a dull (and stressed!) boy!

Multiple Choice

1. What are some of the signs of stress?

   a) Having trouble sleeping.
   b) Losing a lot of weight.
   c) Having trouble concentrating.
   d) All of the above.

2. Which is not a cause of stress?

   a) Driving in heavy traffic.
   b) Getting good grades at school.
   c) Losing your job.
   d) Breaking up with your boyfriend.

3. What is something we can do to lower stress?

   a) Drink more coffee or tea.
   b) Eat a lot of candy and cakes.
   c) Exercise.
   d) Do poorly at school.

Vocabulary Activity

Look at the words below that describe symptoms of stress, why stress happens or possible remedies for stress. Place them into one of the three columns. Then, try to think of two or three other things that could go into each column.

meditation / lower back pain / being hurried / gained a lot of weight / find time to relax / driving in heavy traffic / doing poorly at school / diarrhea / frequent headaches / drink less coffee / trouble sleeping / breaking up with a boy or girlfriend / playing a sport / eating right / trouble concentrating

Symptoms	Why Stress Happens	Possible Remedies

Discussion Questions

What are the things that make you feel stress? What do you do to reduce stress?

Visiting A Doctor

Most people will need to visit a doctor at some point in their lives. While doctors want to help us, there are a few ways that we can make their job easier and can help ourselves. One of the best ways to help ourselves and make their job easier is by being honest with the doctor. Try to answer all of the doctor's questions, even if revealing the answers may make you uncomfortable. Other ways to help yourself are by communicating clearly with a doctor and fully understanding a doctor's advice.

It is very important to communicate clearly with your doctor. Be prepared to answer questions about any diseases that you or other family members have or have had and of any allergies you may have. You should also try to explain as best as you can about what is ailing you. Try to explain when you became sick, why you think you are sick, and what symptoms you have. Also, your doctor may ask you to describe your daily habits. Try to be very specific when you answer the doctor's questions.

You should be certain that you understand your doctor's instructions on what to do to get better. After a doctor has examined you, he will explain your condition and give you advice about how to treat it. He may also prescribe certain drugs. When he explains these things, make sure that you are certain of what you need to do and why it is important. If you have any questions or concerns, be sure to ask the doctor. Of course, after the doctor has given you advice, follow it!

Doctors want to help their patients. They have studied for years to be able to treat you. Doctors need your help to do their job properly.

Multiple Choice

1. The main idea of this reading is...

    a) do not go to a doctor.
    b) doctors go to school.
    c) communicate clearly with a doctor.

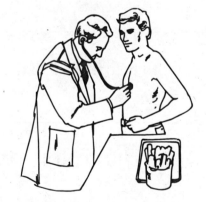

2. Which of the following is NOT a good idea...

    a) explaining your sickness clearly.   b) listening to a doctor.   c) lying to a doctor.

3. It is important to tell a doctor about your family's health because...

    a) the doctor wants more patients.
    b) you may have a similar problem.
    c) none of these.

Mistakes

Explain which mistake each of these people made:

1. John took medicine to which he was allergic. He forgot to _____

2. Jane does not understand the medicines she must take. She forgot to _____

3. Jack did not tell the doctor what he ate last night because he was embarrassed.
   Jack should have been _____

Your & Their

We use YOUR and THEIR to show possession. Examples:

Most people will need to visit a doctor at some point in THEIR lives. (THEIR lives is the same as THE LIVES THAT PEOPLE HAVE.)

The doctor may ask you to describe YOUR daily habits. (YOUR daily habits is the same as THE DAILY HABITS YOU HAVE)

Use YOUR and THEIR to express each of the sentences below more clearly.

1. You should be certain you understand THE INSTRUCTIONS YOU HAVE from the doctor.

_____.

2. Doctors want to help THE PATIENTS THAT THEY HAVE.

_____.

3. He will explain THE CONDITION THAT YOU HAVE.

_____.

4. Doctors need HELP THAT YOU HAVE to do THE JOB THAT THEY HAVE properly.

_____.

The ABCs Of Fire Extinguishers

The first thing to remember about fire extinguishers is that they are meant for small fires only! If you have a fire in your home, the two most important things to do are to get everybody out of the house and to call the fire department (or 911). Then, and only then, if you think you can put the fire out, use the fire extinguisher.

There are different kinds of fires that happen in the home. For example, there are fires that burn materials like wood, paper and curtains. Another kind of fire involves liquids like gasoline, fuel oil and paint solvents. In addition, there is a type of fire that involves electrical equipment. Finally, there are fires in the kitchen that happen while cooking and these involve grease or oil. Different kinds of fires need different fire extinguishers. To be safe, you need to have at least four fire extinguishers; one for each of these four types of home fires. Remember that using the wrong extinguisher can make the fire worse.

You also need to know how to use the fire extinguisher. Remember the word "P.A.S.S.". "P" is for pull the pin. "A" is aim the fire extinguisher at the base of the flames. A common mistake is aiming at the flames, but by doing this you end up shooting over the fire. "S" is for squeeze the trigger and the last "S" is for sweep the fire extinguisher from side to side.

Although fire extinguishers are very useful and can help save property, do not forget to always save people first!

Multiple Choice

1. What are the two most important things to do if you have a fire?

   a) Try to put it out with the fire extinguisher.
   b) Get everybody out of the house.
   c) Call the fire department or 911.
   d) a and b.
   e) b and c.

2. There are generally how many types of home fires?

   a) Two.   b) Four.   c) Eight.

3. When using a fire extinguisher you should NOT...

   a) sweep the extinguisher from side to side.
   b) aim the extinguisher at the base of the flames.
   c) aim the extinguisher at the highest point of the flame.

What Is The Right Order?

If there was fire in your house, in what order would you do the following things.

_____ Squeeze the trigger of the fire extinguisher.

_____ Call the fire department or 911.

_____ Pull the pin of the fire extinguisher.

_____ If you think you can put the fire out without hurting yourself, get the fire extinguisher.

_____ Aim the fire extinguisher at the base of the flames.

_____ Sweep the fire extinguisher from side to side.

_____ Get everybody out of the house safely.

Summarizing Information

Choose the best summary for each paragraph. Put summary letters in the correct spaces. Of the six (6) summaries, only four (4) can be used.

Paragraph 1 talks about _____   Paragraph 2 talks about _____

Paragraph 3 talks about _____   Paragraph 4 talks about _____

a) The most important things to remember if there is a fire.

b) How not to use a fire extinguisher.

c) Fire extinguishers are useful, but remember to save people first.

d) A word to remember when using a fire extinguisher.

e) Prevention is the most important thing of all.

f) The different kinds of fires that can happen in your home.

Related Activity

Make a list of three places you could go to find out more information about the different kinds of fires and the fire extinguishers that are needed to put them out.

Drowning Prevention

Many people die from drowning each year. Quite often, the victims knew how to swim. If you do not know how to swim or how to help someone who is drowning, you should learn. In most towns or cities there are free or inexpensive classes in water safety. Three ways to help prevent drowning are to wear a life jacket, know the water, and know your own abilities.

Life jackets save lives. If you get on a small boat, it is a very good idea to wear a life jacket even if you know how to swim. Sometimes when a person falls out of a boat, they may be injured by an accident and unable to swim or the water may be too fast for a person to swim to safety. Also, small children near open water should wear a life jacket.

It helps to know the water where you swim or boat. Obey safe boating procedures. If you swim in a lake or river, understand that it is more difficult than swimming in a pool. In all circumstances know how cold the water is, how deep it is, and how fast it moves. Remember that water in a lake or river moves much faster than it appears to move. Also, understand that the water can become deep or shallow very suddenly so watch out for rocks or other obstacles.

Of course, it is important to know how far you can swim. Many people think they can swim longer distances than they really can. In addition, when you look across water, many objects look closer than what they really are. Test your swimming ability in a safe place where you can stop before you try swimming long distances on open water. Also learn how to rest in the water by floating or changing strokes. If someone appears to be drowning, always help the person. Some people have drowned while people stood by because they thought the person was joking or pretending.

Swimming and boating can be good exercise and a lot of fun. Just remember that safety comes first.

Multiple Choice

1. If you do not know how to swim you should...

   a) learn on your own.
   b) take a swimming class.
   c) wait until you need it.

2. People should wear a life jacket in a boat even if they know how to swim because...

   a) the water may be too fast or cold for them.   b) they may be injured.   c) both of these.

3) Before you swim in a lake or river...

a) know about its temperature and speed.   b) take a shower.   c) push your friend in first.

Vocabulary

Below are three (3) definitions. Which word from the story does each define?

1. To die below water: _____

2. Equipment that can help a person float: _____

3. A way to rest in water: _____

Minimal Pairs

Minimal pairs are two words that have only one letter different. Their meanings are often very different.

For example, the words CAT and COT have only one letter different. However, they have very different meanings.

We can NEVER say: The cot ate a mouse.

                        or

                        A soldier sleeps on a cat.

Each sentence below has a mistake with a minimal pair. Circle the word that does not belong and then write the correct word in the space provided.

1. Swimming in a like is more difficult than swimming in a pool. _____

2. You should wear a life jacket in a small boat because you may fill out. _____

3. If you swim in a river, be careful of racks. _____

4. Deer water can be dangerous if you cannot swim. _____

5. Swimming and boating can be fan but we should always be safe. _____

Tornadoes

In January 1974, a tornado in McComb, Mississippi picked up three school buses and threw them over an eight-foot wall. An unusually strong tornado on April 8, 1998 in Birmingham, Alabama picked up things that were carried over 100 miles before they fell to the ground. A tornado is a violent wind storm that is shaped like a funnel. Tornadoes, or twisters as they are sometimes called, can do amazing things.

Tornadoes have wind speeds that can be more than 200 miles per hour (321 kilometers per hour). Although most tornadoes last less than an hour, some can last several hours. On the average, tornadoes travel a distance of about 20 miles. We usually see tornadoes on hot, humid days in the afternoon or early evening in the spring.

If a tornado is near you, you should go to the basement of your house or the building you are in. Stay away from windows and open places. Also, stay away from places that have large roofs, like cafeterias, auditoriums and gymnasiums. If possible, try to get under a heavy piece of furniture, like a table or desk, and hold onto it. If you cannot find a strong piece of furniture, sit on the floor, put your head between your knees and then cover your head with your arms. Do not leave until you are sure the tornado has passed. Although tornadoes can be very dangerous, the good news is that they often pass quickly and that especially strong tornadoes are rare.

Multiple Choice

1. Tornadoes are often called...

   a) hurricanes.
   b) twisters.
   c) earthquakes.

2. Generally, we see tornadoes on...

   a) cold and snowy evenings in the winter.
   b) warm and rainy afternoons in the fall.
   c) hot and humid afternoons in the spring.

3. If a tornado is near, you should...

   a) go to the school's cafeteria or gymnasium.
   b) try to get under a heavy table or desk.
   c) stand near a window.

Correct The Mistakes

Find the mistakes in the following sentences. Rewrite the sentences correctly.

1. In January 1974, a tornado in McComb, Mississippi picked up three taxi cabs and threw them over an eight-foot wall.

_____.

2. An unusually strong tornado in Birmingham, Georgia in 1998 picked up things that were carried over 100 miles before they fell to the ground.

_____.

3. Most tornadoes last less than an hour, but some can last several days.

_____.

4. Tornadoes have wind speeds that can be more than 300 miles per hour (482 kilometers per hour).

_____.

5. If a tornado is near you, you should go to places that have large roofs, like cafeterias, auditoriums and gymnasiums.

_____.

6. If it is possible, try to sit on top of a heavy piece of furniture, like a table or desk.

_____.

Discussion Questions

What is the biggest storm you can remember experiencing yourself? What kind of storm was it? Where did it occur? When did it occur? Describe it.

Automobile Maintenance

Cars kill more people in a year than any other mode of transportation. Some accidents can be prevented if a car is running properly. Most states or provinces require that cars have some basic safety features. Be sure to understand what your car is required to have. If you have any questions, talk to a mechanic. A mechanic can normally inspect your car and explain what is needed for it to be safe. Many times, it is easy and inexpensive to make your car safe.

For example, your car has many different kinds of lights. You need all of them working properly to be safe. The car should have at least two headlights, two taillights and two turn signals. You need taillights and turn signals because if other cars do not know when you will brake or when you will turn, it may cause an accident. If you drive at night or in dangerous weather without headlights that work properly, this may also cause an accident. If you notice that your lights do not work, go to a mechanic immediately.

You should also make sure that your tires are safe. They should have enough air in them at all times and they should have enough tread to keep the car on the road. It is a good idea to check your tires often. If you notice the car's tires making strange sounds or that the car seems to move sharply to the left or right, ask a mechanic to check them.

Almost any driver can make sure that the car's windows and mirrors are clean and unobstructed. You should be able to see in front of the car, behind it, and on both sides. Many accidents occur when a driver's view is blocked.

Your car is a complex machine, so you should spend the time it takes to make sure that it is safe to drive. In the end, it is far more convenient to keep your car safe than it is to have an accident.

Multiple Choice

1. Cars can be dangerous to drive when...

   a) the lights do not work.
   b) the tires do not have enough air.
   c) the windows are blocked.
   d) all of these.

2. You notice that the car keeps moving to one side of the road. You should...

   a) buy a new car.   b) check the tires.   c) turn on the lights.   d) none of these.

3. Most states and provinces...

   a) require cars to be safe to drive. b) are not interested in auto maintenance.
   c) only worry when you have an accident. d) all of these.

Matching

Match the following problems and solutions.

1. check the tires   a. you get a fine for your car maintenance

2. check the car's lights   b. you cannot see what is in front of you

3. clean the windshield   c. cars do not slow down when you turn

4. learn the laws in your state/province   d. your cars is hard to control

Quantifiers

Quantifiers are words that indicate an amount.

    For example: An automobile has TWO headlights.

However, we also use other words that are not numbers to indicate an amount.

    For example: It often takes LESS time to repair a car than the time it takes to recover from an accident.

Find the missing letters to complete the following quantifiers. All of them are in the reading.

1.   ____ o ____ e

2.   ____ o m ____

3.   a ____   ____ e a ____ ____ (two words)

4.   ____ a ____ ____

5.   e ____ o u ____ ____

6.   ____ o ____ ____

The Fight Against Cancer

Cancer is a serious disease where the cells of the body increase rapidly and in an uncontrolled way. This year over one half million North Americans will die from cancer. One out of four deaths in North America is from cancer and it is the second leading cause of death, only heart disease kills more people. There are many different kinds of cancer and its cause can be both internal and external. The good news is that we are not helpless in the fight against cancer. There are many things we can do to reduce our chances of getting cancer.

One-third of cancer deaths is from cigarette smoking. Another third is from having a poor diet, including eating too many foods that make us obese: extremely overweight. We can lower our chances of getting cancer by making three choices: the first is to not smoke, the second is to eat a healthy diet and the third is to exercise regularly.

One of the most common forms of cancer is skin cancer, over a million new cases are diagnosed each year. Skin cancer is more common than organ cancers, such as liver, lung, prostate or stomach. Most cases of skin cancer are caused by the ultraviolet (UV) rays of sunlight. To protect yourself from UV rays try not to be in direct sunlight between 10:00 a.m. and 3:00 p.m. Also, it is always a good idea to put on a sunscreen before going out in the sun.

Another thing we can do in the fight against cancer is to discover it in its early stages. Be knowledgeable about your own health, either by self-examinations or through examinations by a health care professional. Remember that the more we know about cancer--the ways to avoid getting it and the ways to detect it in its early stages--the more successful we will be in staying healthy.

Multiple Choice

1. What is the most common form of cancer?

   a) Lung.
   b) Prostate.
   c) Skin.

2. One third of cancer deaths is from...

   a) cigarette smoking.
   b) skin cancer.
   c) liver cancer.   d) a and c   e) all of the above.

3. The good news is that...

   a) there are many things we can do to reduce our chances of getting cancer.
   b) there may be a cure for cancer in the next five or ten years.
   c) cancer is only the second leading cause of death in North America.

Match The Sentence Parts

_____   1. Skin cancer is more common than organ cancers...

_____   2. It is always a good idea to put on sunscreen...

_____   3. A third of cancer deaths are from having a poor diet...

_____   4. The more we know about cancer...

a. the more successful we will be in fighting it.
b. such as liver, lungs, prostate or stomach.
c. including eating foods that make us fat.
d. before going out in the direct sunlight.

Summarizing Information

Choose the best summary for each paragraph. Put summary letters in the correct spaces. Of the six summaries (6), only four (4) can be used.

Paragraph 1 talks about _____   Paragraph 2 talks about _____

Paragraph 3 talks about _____   Paragraph 4 talks about _____

a) How to conduct a self-examination.

b) How knowledge about cancer helps in the fight against the disease.

c) How cancer is treated by health care professionals.

d) Cigarette smoking, a bad diet, and ways to reduce the risk of getting cancer.

e) What cancer is.

f) Skin cancer.

The Main Idea

The main idea of this article is that...

a) skin cancer is the most common form of cancer.
b) there are steps that can be taken to reduce your chances of getting cancer.
c) cancer is the second leading cause of death in North America.

Dealing With The Police

You are walking or driving down the street when a police officer drives past you and stops you...What should you do or say? Most law enforcement officers are well trained; they will try to help and protect you. They do not want to hurt or injure you. However, if they feel that they or someone else is in danger, they must try to defend themselves. There are a few actions that can keep you safe if the police confront you.

First of all, stay calm. Do not shout at the police or threaten them. Try to answer their questions and follow any instructions they give you. If you think that the police officer has made a mistake, attempt to explain yourself to them as clearly as possible.

Second, do not make any quick movements with your hands. A police officer may think that you are carrying a weapon. Put your hands where the police officer tells you. Be especially careful about reaching inside a pocket or a coat. Before you do these things, tell the officer what you are doing.

Finally, do not try to run. If the police think that you have committed a serious crime, ask for permission to call a lawyer. By running, you will only make your situation more difficult and more dangerous.

Police officers are professionals who try to do a good job. Most of them would never hurt anyone. However, they are human. Like all human beings, they want to feel secure. It is better for everyone if we treat police officers with the respect that they deserve.

Multiple Choice

1. If a police officers stops you...

   a) shout at them.
   b) run away.
   c) follow their directions.
   d) wave your hands.

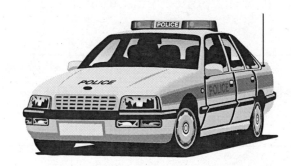

2. If a police officer thinks that you are a criminal you should...

   a) ask for a lawyer. b) confess to the crime. c) threaten to have him fired. d) cry.

3. You do NOT want a police officer to feel...

   a) respect for you. b) calm. c) afraid for himself or someone else. d) confident.

Fill In The Blanks

Complete each sentence below.

1. A police officer does not want to _____.

2. You should always _____ any instructions a police officer gives you.

3. If a police officer wants to arrest you for a serious crime, always call _____.

Do & Does In Negative Sentences

If we want to make a sentence negative we will often use the word DO or the word DOES with the word NOT.

    Examples: Run from a police officer.
                    DO NOT run from a police officer.

                    A police officer wants to arrest an innocent person.
                    A police officer DOES NOT want to arrest an innocent person.

Make each sentence below negative.

1. Shout at the police and threaten them.

_____.

2. Make quick or sudden movements.

_____.

3. A police officer wants to hurt you.

_____.

4. A police officer wants to let the bad guys get away.

_____.

5. Hit a police officer.

_____.

The Heimlich Maneuver

A person who is choking cannot breathe or speak. After a short time, the person's face will turn purple or blue and then he or she will faint. If the object that is stuck in the person's throat is not removed, the person could die in 4 to 6 minutes. If you see someone choking, it is important to take fast action. The Heimlich Maneuver is an excellent way to help someone who is choking.

To do the Heimlich Maneuver you need to stand behind the person and then put your arms around his or her waist. Make a fist with one hand and then place the fist against the person's stomach, a little below the ribs, but above the navel. Take your other hand and hold the fist. Then with your arms around the person, pull up and inward quickly. If done correctly, the Heimlich Maneuver will force air out of the person's lungs and the air pressure will blow the object out of the person's throat.

If a baby is choking, hold the baby face down on your lap. The head should be a little lower than the rest of the body. Give the baby four sharp hits with the heel of your hand on the back. If this does not work, turn the baby face up and give four sharp pushes to the chest, as you would do for someone suffering from a heart attack.

You can learn the Heimlich Maneuver properly by taking a class. Contact your local public health organization to locate a first aid course in your town.

Multiple Choice

1. To do the Heimlich Maneuver you first need to...

    a) have the person who is choking lie down.
    b) stand behind the person who is choking and put your arms around him or her.
    c) find out what the person was eating.

2. If the Heimlich Maneuver is done correctly...

    a) air will force the object out of the person's throat.
    b) the person who is choking will blow at the object.
    c) it can cause a heart attack.

3. One of the best ways to learn more about the Heimlich Maneuver is to...

    a) practice it at home.
    b) try it out when you see someone choking.
    c) take a course in first aid.

Summarizing Information

Choose the best summary for each paragraph. Put summary letters in the correct spaces. Of the six (6) summaries, only four (4) can be used.

Paragraph 1 talks about _____

Paragraph 2 talks about _____

Paragraph 3 talks about _____

Paragraph 4 talks about _____

a) How to perform the Heimlich Maneuver.

b) How to treat choking babies.

c) The similarities between the Heimlich Maneuver and treating someone who has suffered a heart attack.

d) What happens when someone is choking.

e) Where you can learn the Heimlich Maneuver.

f) Foods that often cause choking.

Discussion Questions

Although Dr. Henry Heimlich has invented several life-saving techniques like the Heimlich Chest Valve and the Heimlich Micro Trach, he is most famous for inventing the Heimlich Maneuver. It is often said that Dr. Heimlich has saved more lives than anyone else. Do you agree or disagree? Can you think of other doctors, inventors or scientists who have also saved many lives? Who has saved the most lives?

Product Labels And Expiration Dates

We can often avoid serious illness by storing food properly, ensuring that it is fresh when we eat it, and understanding what the product contains. The easiest way to accomplish this is to read a product's label.

If you eat or drink something that is spoiled, you could become sick. If you have a high fever, begin to vomit, or have diarrhea for several hours without getting better, you should go to a doctor. Be especially concerned with very young children or elderly people.

You should be very careful about how you store certain foods. When you buy milk or meat at the store, be sure that it is unopened. If meat is not wrapped tightly or if a milk carton is open, do not buy it. After you buy milk, meat, or fish, put it in a refrigerator as soon as possible. Be especially diligent on hot days. Before you cook meat or fish, or drink milk, be sure that it smells the way it should and that its color is normal.

It is always a good idea to know how fresh the products are when you buy them, especially with dairy products, seafood, and meat. These products are required to have an expiration date. In other words, there should be a date stamped on a milk carton and on most meat packages. For example, if a product's expiration date is January 5, it should not be consumed on January 6. Other products like bread or cereal may also have expiration dates.

For some people, it is important to read a product's label to understand what that product contains. Under certain medical conditions, a doctor may advise someone to avoid salt, sugar, caffeine, or other substances that may be harmful. A doctor or dietician may also ask a patient to eat foods which have certain substances that their bodies need. If you have questions, ask a doctor or a dietician about what words to look for.

We all have to eat! We just need to be sure that the food we eat will make us happy and healthy. Read the label!

Multiple Choice

1. Which product listed below seems like the safest purchase?

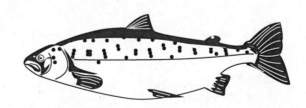

   a) Red meat that is brown.
   b) A package that is open.
   c) Milk that expires in 15 days.

2. An important thing to remember about food is...

   a) it should be consumed before it reaches its expiration date.
   b) it should be stored properly.
   c) always read the label.
   d) keep fish, meat and milk in the refrigerator until you are ready to use them.
   e) all of the above.

Finding Examples

Your doctor told you not to eat or drink products with caffeine. List three (3) or more products you should avoid.

1. _____

2. _____

3. _____

It

We use the pronoun IT as both a subject and as an object.

Example of IT used as a subject:

IT is always a good idea to know how fresh the products are when you buy them.

Example of IT used as an object:

If a milk carton is open, do not buy IT.

In the reading, find 2 examples of IT used as a subject and 2 examples of IT used as an object.

IT used as a Subject:

1. _____

2. _____

IT used as an Object:

1. _____

2. _____

The Internet

All over the world, more and more people are going "online". The Internet, or World Wide Web (WWW), can be educational and fun, but at the same time, we must pay attention to the possible dangers of "surfing the Web". Young people should be especially careful. Here are some things that youths can do to have a safe and pleasant Internet experience.

Be careful of strangers. While "chat rooms" let people from all over the world meet and talk, be careful of someone who wants something from you or uses language that makes you uncomfortable. If this happens, you should log off. Never give anyone your real last name, address or telephone number. If someone asks you for this information, log off immediately. Never make plans to meet someone that you have met on the Internet without telling your parents first.

As a parent, there are several things you can do to make sure that your child's Internet experiences are good ones. First, if you are just starting out, you should find out what the Internet is all about by researching the subject at a library or by taking a computer course. Next, parents should spend time with their children while they are on the Internet. Parents need to know what are the websites that their children are visiting when they go online. While you can buy programs that will "block" your child's ability to go to certain places on the Internet, the most important thing for you to do is to keep an open channel of communication with your child.

Multiple Choice

1. WWW stands for...

   a) World Wide Wait.
   b) Wave World Wide.
   c) World Wide Web.

2. If you are in a chat room and someone asks you for your last name and address, you should...

   a) ask the person why he or she wants to know.
   b) log off immediately.
   c) give your last name, but not your address.

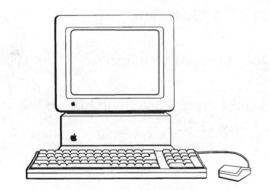

3. Circle two things that you should do as a parent to protect your children when they go online...

   a) find out about the Internet if you do not know what it is.
   b) spend at least two hours a day surfing the web.
   c) talk to your children about the Internet and spend some time with them when they go online.

Vocabulary Of The Internet

_____   1. surfing the web

_____   2. log on/off the Internet

_____   3. chat room

_____   4. blocking

a. a place where people can meet and "talk" to each other through their computers
b. to go from place to place on the Internet
c. to stop someone from going to certain places on the Internet
d. getting on or off the World Wide Web

Website Design

With a classmate or in a group, on paper, design a one or two page website. Your website can be for your class, your school, a pretend company, or anything that pleases you and your partners. Show your website to your classmates.

Discussion Questions

1. Do you surf the Internet? What types of websites do you visit?

2. Should there be censorship on the Internet? Whose responsibility is it to "police" the World Wide Web?

Boating Safety

Many people enjoy using boats. There are many different kinds of boats to use and many different places to use them. Before you take a boat in open water, there are things you must know. Probably the most important thing is to know the regulations in your area. Most provinces and states have laws about how to use a boat, where to use it, and what the boat should be equipped with. Before you take your boat ride, learn these laws and follow them. The rules are there to help you. It is a good idea to take a boating safety course. Most boating organizations or the Coast Guard can help you find a course near you.

All boaters should keep three things in mind before any trip: life preservers, sobriety, and preparation. In other words, every person on the boat should have a life jacket. Life jackets will keep a person afloat if they fall out of the boat. Even strong swimmers should have a life preserver because a person may be injured or unconscious after a fall from a boat. Also, it is a fact that most boating accidents occur when someone driving a boat has been drinking alcohol. Do not allow anyone to drink even one alcoholic drink and drive a boat. Obviously, good preparation is essential. The boat should be in good condition. Make sure that the motor has enough fuel and that it works well before you leave.

There are also a few supplies that should be on the boat. First of all, a boat should have a radio with extra batteries. A radio can keep you informed of any changes in the weather. Also, a first aid kit is a good idea and a flashlight with extra batteries may be very useful, especially if you are going to be boating at night. Local laws may require a boat to have other equipment, so be aware of what is required.

Of course, it is a good idea to tell someone where you are going and when you expect to be back. Make sure that this person knows what kind of boat you have, and how many people are with you. This person should also know who to call if you do not arrive back to shore when expected.

There is no doubt that boating is an enjoyable activity. Remember, the more you prepare for your boat trip, the more enjoyment awaits you out on the water.

Multiple Choice

1. Before you use a boat on open water...

    a) learn about boating regulations.
    b) take a boating safety course.
    c) both of these.

2. If you are a good swimmer you should...

    a) leave your life jacket at home.
    b) wear a life jacket.
    c) have it in the boat, but not wear it.

Sentence Completions

Complete each of the following sentences.

1. Boaters should never drink alcohol because _____

_____.

2. Boaters should tell someone about their plans because _____

_____.

3. Boaters should carry a radio because _____

_____.

Commands

We give commands in English by using a verb without a subject.

    Examples:

        LEARN the law.
        FOLLOW the law.

Give a command for each situation below by completing each sentence.

1. Your friend is taking a 2-day boat trip. You notice that he does not have a radio.

    Take _____.

2. You see someone begin to operate a boat. You notice that she has a beer in her hand.

    Do not _____.

3. Your brother wants to buy a boat. He is not aware of his province's boating rules.

    Learn _____.

Tips For Babysitters

Babysitters have one great responsibility: the safety of the children in their care. Babysitters need to be prepared while they are watching children. There are several ways for them to be ready for this important job.

The first way to prepare a babysitter is to supply him or her with written information. Parents should write down their names, the children's names, the house address (with nearest cross street) and the house phone number and then give this list to the babysitter. This list should also include the telephone number where they can be reached and also the number of a close relative or neighbor, as well as the family doctor's telephone number. Parents should see if there is a poison control center in their area and leave that number too. Finally, the number for emergencies should be at the top of the list: 911.

Before the parents leave, they should make certain the babysitter is familiar with the house and knows which doors and windows can be used as an emergency exit. Parents also need to show the babysitter the swimming pool, if there is one, and any areas where they keep things that could be dangerous for children, such as matches, plastic bags and medicine. After the parents leave, the babysitter needs to know where the children are at all times. Even if the children are sleeping, the babysitter should check on them every 15 minutes. It is not a good idea for the babysitter to have visitors, and if the babysitter intends to do so he or she should always ask the homeowners beforehand if it is permitted.

If there is a fire, the most important thing is to get everybody safely out of the house. Do not try to go back inside for any reason! Always remember that safety is the most important thing to keep in mind while babysitting.

Multiple Choice

1. Parents should prepare a babysitter by...

   a) leaving snack foods for the babysitter.
   b) leaving all the necessary important
      information the babysitter may need.
   c) showing the babysitter how to operate the
      DVD player.

2. Which are examples of dangerous things that
   are found in a house that parents need to
   show babysitters before leaving?

   a) Pens, paper and notebooks.   b) Refrigerator, telephone and television.
   c) Plastic bags, medicine and matches.

3. Why is babysitting such a great responsibility?

   a) Babysitters are responsible for the safety of the children they are babysitting.
   b) Babysitters must know which television programs the children like the most.

Summarizing Information

Choose the best summary for each paragraph. Put summary letters in the correct spaces. Of the six (6) summaries, only four (4) can be used.

Paragraph 1 talks about _____

Paragraph 2 talks about _____

Paragraph 3 talks about _____

Paragraph 4 talks about _____

a) What to do if there is a fire while you are babysitting.

b) The number of visitors babysitters should invite to visit while the children sleep.

c) A babysitters greatest responsibility.

d) Informing the babysitter about the house, dangerous things and whether visitors are allowed.

e) The list of important numbers and things parents should leave with their babysitter.

f) Ways a babysitter can entertain children.

Related Activities

1. Make a list of all the telephone numbers mentioned in the story that parents should give the babysitter.

2. Make a floor plan of the house or apartment where you live. Draw all the possible ways that you could escape if there was a fire. Mark the doors or windows that you could not escape from.

3. Look in the telephone book or call information and find where is the nearest poison control center. Write down the telephone number and share it with the other members of your class.

Immunizations

Immunizations or vaccines are very important to be healthy. Immunizations and vaccines are a group of medicines that may prevent a person from getting serious diseases, especially diseases that pass from one person to another. Some immunizations need to be given to infants, others need to be given to adults, and some need to be given to people traveling to certain countries. Most health departments, hospitals, and doctors can give you more information.

Babies and young children should have a series of immunizations. Most of these require that they get an injection. It is important that children understand that these shots are important for their health and that they should be brave, even when the needle hurts. The number and kind of shots that children need may change as doctors learn more about how to prevent these diseases. Your health care professional will know what kinds of vaccinations are needed. Many times, schools will not allow children to attend without certain vaccinations. Vaccinations for children may include shots for polio, mumps and measles.

Adults also need to have some vaccinations, especially if they did not have them as children. It is probably a good idea to have immunizations for tetanus and diphtheria. Most people should probably have these shots at least once every 10 years. Also, people who travel to or from certain countries may need other kinds of vaccinations. Before you travel to another country, it is a good idea to ask a doctor what kinds of vaccinations he or she recommends.

There is a famous saying: No pain, no gain. Most people are uncomfortable about having injections. However, most doctors would say that the pain from a shot disappears much faster than the pain from a serious disease.

Multiple Choice

1. Where can you find more information about immunizations?

   a) At a doctor's office.
   b) At the health department.
   c) At a hospital.
   d) All of the above.

2. Immunizations can help adults and children...

   a) give a disease to their friends.   b) prevent all diseases.
   c) prevent us from having many serious diseases.

3. Many people do not like to get a vaccination because...

   a) they taste bad.   b) they are dangerous.   c) the shot hurts.

Remembering Details

List three (3) diseases that immunizations can prevent.

1. _____

2. _____

3. _____

Corrections

The paragraph below has 5 mistakes. All of the mistakes are incorrect information. Find and underline the incorrect information and write the correct information in the spaces provided below.

Babies and young children should have a series of immunizations. Most of these require that they get an injection. It is important that children ignore these shots that are important for their fun and that they should be brave, even when the needle hurts. The number and kind of shots that children want may change as doctors learn more about how to prevent these diseases. Your health care professional will know what kinds of vaccinations are unneeded. Many times, schools will not allow children to attend without certain vaccinations. Vaccinations for children may include shots for polio, colds and measles.

1. _____

2. _____

3. _____

4. _____

5. _____

The School Bus

More than twenty-five million students in North America use a school bus to go to and from school each day. Surprisingly, the greatest danger for students is not riding the bus, but instead the greatest danger for students is the time immediately before boarding the bus and the time immediately after exiting the bus.

If you are a student, you should get to the bus stop at least five minutes before the bus arrives and stand at least six feet (1.82 meters) away from the curb. If the bus is stopped and you have to cross the street in front of the bus, you should cross at least 10 feet (3.04 meters) in front of it so the bus driver can see you. When getting on the bus, wait until the doors are completely open and the driver says that you may enter. Never walk behind the bus or try to pick something up that you have dropped near the bus. If you have dropped something near or under the bus, always tell the bus driver before you try to get it.

If you are an automobile or truck driver, you need to be alert for students arriving at and leaving their bus, especially when you are driving in school zones. Pay special attention during the hours that students go to and return from school. Even as a car or truck driver you need to know the school bus laws in your state or province.

If you are a parent, you need to teach your children about school bus safety so that their daily trip to school is a safe one.

Multiple Choice

1. For students who use a school bus, the least dangerous part of their daily trip is...

    a) riding the bus.
    b) coming to the bus.
    c) leaving the bus.

2. If you drop something and it falls under the bus, you should...

    a) try to get it as quickly as possible.
    b) leave it under the bus and go home.
    c) tell the bus driver what happened.

3. Which of the following is NOT a safe thing to do?

    a) Learn about the bus safety laws of your state or province.
    b) Try to get to the bus stop at exactly the time as the bus arrives.
    c) Talk to your child about school bus safety.

Matching The Numbers

_____   1. 10 feet (3.04 meters)

_____   2. 6 feet (1.82 meters)

_____   3. over 25 million

_____   4. at least 5 minutes

a. The number of students who ride a school bus to school each day.
b. How far away a student should be when crossing in front of a stopped bus.
c. How far away from the curb a student should be when waiting for the bus.
d. How long a student should be at the bus stop before the bus comes.

Summarizing Information

Choose the best summary for each paragraph. Put summary letters in the correct spaces. Of the six (6) summaries, only four (4) can be used.

Paragraph 1 talks about _____   Paragraph 2 talks about _____

Paragraph 3 talks about _____   Paragraph 4 talks about _____

a) School bus accidents.

b) How to wait for the school bus.

c) The responsibilities of other drivers concerning school buses.

d) Safety tips for school bus riders.

e) The greatest danger facing students who ride a school bus.

f) A parent's responsibility regarding school bus safety.

Swimming Pool Safety

Swimming pools can be a good source of fun and exercise. There are many public and private organizations that offer swimming classes. If you are interested in learning how to swim, call one of them. However, if you go to a friend's house, you need to understand how to be safe. Pools can be especially dangerous for non-swimmers and young children.

The first rule to remember about using a swimming pool safely is to never swim alone. Even an experienced swimmer will need help sometimes. If children are around be sure that they understand that there should be an adult present who knows how to swim. It is also a good idea to tell them to stay in the shallow end of the pool and use a "buddy system". In other words, there should be one other person who always knows where you are, and you should also be responsible for at least one other person.

Second, remember that many accidents happen around the pool. Be very careful getting in and out of a pool and always walk to its edge. In addition, you should be very careful jumping or diving into a pool. Make sure that the water is deep enough and that there is no one near you when you jump.

Finally, most people who follow these simple rules will be very safe. However, make sure that everyone knows what to do if a swimmer has a problem. Everyone in the pool should know where the life buoy is. A life buoy is equipment that a person can hold on to and float. Most life buoys are tied to a rope. (Obviously, every pool should have a life buoy!). If you see that a person is in trouble, throw the life buoy to them and pull them to the side of the pool with the rope. If the person is seriously injured, call 911.

Pools are great places to meet new people and learn new skills. Just follow a few simple rules, and enjoy!

Multiple Choice

1. The main idea of this reading is that you should...

    a) never swim in a pool.
    b) follow a few easy rules when you swim.
    c) buy a pool.

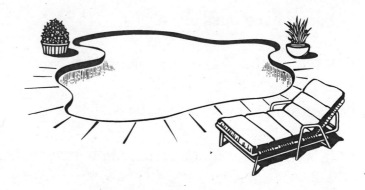

2. The "buddy system" means that...

    a) you should never dive in the shallow end. b) never swim alone. c) learn to swim.

3. Every pool should have a...

    a) deep end. b) diving board. c) "buddy system". d) life buoy.

Vocabulary Practice

Draw a line to match each of the words on the left below with its definition on the right.

1. life buoy   a. a person who cannot swim

2. buddy system   b. an area with water that is not deep

3. shallow end   c. equipment that helps a swimmer

4. non-swimmer   d. a way know where everyone is

Summarizing Information

Choose the best summary for each paragraph. Put summary letters in the correct spaces. Of the seven (7) summaries, only five (5) can be used.

Paragraph 1 talks about _____

Paragraph 2 talks about _____

Paragraph 3 talks about _____

Paragraph 4 talks about _____

Paragraph 5 talks about _____

a) Pools are fun, but follow the rules.

b) Learning to swim is easy.

c) It is important to understand how to be safe around swimming pools.

d) Life saving equipment that should be near a pool.

e) How deep a pool should be filled.

f) Only walk around a pool and make sure you know how deep the water is when you jump in.

g) Never swim alone.

Frostbite

Winter can be, with its frozen beauty and snowball-fight fun, a great time for both children and adults, but be careful of some dangers. One of the most dangerous things about winter is the cold, which can cause frostbite. When outside in cold weather, we need to pay special attention to young children since they may not have the vocabulary to tell us they are in distress.

Some warning signs of frostbite are shivering, change of skin color (it becomes either red or very white) and numbness (when you lose feeling in part of your body). If you think you have frostbite, you need to warm the body part, but do not rub it. You can warm the area with lukewarm--but not hot--water. If the pain does not stop, you need to see a doctor.

Frostbite can usually be prevented if the right steps are taken before going outside. It is always best to dress in several lighter layers, rather than one heavy layer. Pay special attention to hands and feet.

Mittens keep hands warmer than gloves and mitten guards for children stop their mittens from being lost. If wet feet is a problem, plastic sacks can be put inside boots to keep feet dry. Also, cream or rubbing oil can be used to protect the face.

Keep in mind that even if dressed correctly, children can be in danger from the cold if they are inactive for a long time; for example, if they are being carried on a parent's back or are riding on a snowmobile. So when winter approaches and the temperature and the snow begin to fall, remember to dress properly and use common sense to protect yourself and any children in your care from winter dangers.

Multiple Choice

1. We need to pay special attention to children in the winter because...

   a) they usually do not like winter as much as adults.
   b) they may not know the right words to say what they are feeling.
   c) they like to have snowball fights.

2. If you think you have frostbite in your hands or feet you should...

   a) put them in water that is just a little bit warm.   b) put them in ice cold water.
   c) rub them.

3. Which of the following is not true?

   a) Plastic sacks inside boots can stop feet from getting wet.
   b) Several light layers of clothing are better than one heavy layer.
   c) Gloves keep hands warmer than mittens.

Correct The Mistake

Find the mistakes in the following sentences. Rewrite the sentences.

1. One warning sign of frostbite is when your skin becomes blue or very white.

_____.

2. Frostbite can rarely be prevented if the right steps are taken before going outside.

_____.

3. Cream or rubbing oil can be used to protect the feet.

_____.

4. Even though they are dressed properly, children may still have problems with the cold if they are active for a long time.

_____.

The Main Idea

The main idea of this article is...

    a. that winter can be safe and we can have a wonderful time if we are careful to guard against its dangers.
    b. what to do if you get frostbite.
    c. that winter is a more dangerous time for children than it is for adults because children do not have the same vocabulary as adults do.

Emergency Evacuation Procedures

There may come a time when you must leave your home quickly because of a dangerous condition such as a hurricane, heavy snow or rain, or an earthquake. If the police or another government agency asks you to leave, then you must do so immediately. In such a situation, there are some ways that you can make an evacuation easier and your home safer. It is always better to be calm and patient during a disaster. Being prepared can help you be both.

Most of the time, public officials will give specific directions about where to go during an emergency. It is often a school, church, or other public building. There you would find shelter, food, and water along with more information about the disaster in progress.

Try to be prepared by knowing what supplies you may need if you are forced to stay away from your home for several days.

Supplies that you may need include medication, important documents, and clothes for 2 or 3 days. It is also smart to have on hand safe drinking water and food that does not need refrigeration. If someone in your family needs prescription medication, then make sure that there is enough available to last a few days. Make sure that you also bring important documents like your driver's license or passport. It is also a good idea to bring any financial and legal documents that you may need later.

Finally, it is wise to secure your home before you leave it. Lock the doors and windows, and write down serial numbers of any valuables that have serial numbers. It is also prudent to have a safe place to lock your other valuable items.

No one wants to see a natural disaster. If they come, then we should try not to make a big problem even worse.

Multiple Choice

1. The best time to evacuate your home is...

   a) 2 or 3 hours after the police tell you.
   b) as soon as the police tell you.
   c) not at all.

2. Which of the following is NOT an important medical supply...

   a) insulin for a diabetic.   b) heart medication.   c) beer for a party.

3. If you have an expensive computer that you cannot take with you...

   a) write down the serial number.   b) destroy it before you leave.   c) stay to protect it.

Definitions

Using your own words and based on information in the article write a definition for each of the following words.

1. evacuation: _____

2. natural disaster: _____

3. supplies: _____

4. secure: _____

5. important documents: _____

If /Then Sentences

Often times when we use the word IF in a sentence we use it to show cause and effect. When we use IF it is to show that IF some condition is met THEN something else will take place.

For example: IF the police ask you to leave, THEN you must leave.

Complete each sentence below using IF or THEN.

1. If a hurricane comes, _____.

2. If someone needs a prescription medication, _____.

3. If your home has expensive things, _____.

4. _____, then it is better to be calm and patient.

5. _____, then we should try not to make the problem even worse.

6. _____, then be prepared by knowing what supplies you may need.

Work Safety Organizations

In North America, there are national organizations that work with both employers and employees to save lives, prevent accidents and protect the health of workers. In the United States, the organization is called The Occupational Safety and Health Administration (OSHA), while in Canada it is the Canadian Center for Occupational Health and Safety (CCOHS).

OSHA was created by the US Congress and has had many success stories in its 30-year history. For example, since 1970 the number of deaths in the workplace has been cut by 74%. OSHA has fought for laws that have almost eliminated brown lung disease--a serious disease that can both disable and kill--in the clothing industry. Accidents and illnesses are usually much lower in industries where OSHA has been able to concentrate its attention. If you have a complaint or a question about your workplace conditions, you can contact your local OSHA office.

In Canada, CCOHS provides useful and important information to both employers and employees. Both CCOHS and OSHA believe a safe and healthy workplace is good not only for employees, but for employers too. Fewer lost workdays and greater productivity are just two ways in which companies profit.

Although these organizations have done much to improve workplace conditions, much work is still to be done before every man and woman has a safe work environment.

Multiple Choice

1. OSHA was created by...

   a) the US Congress.
   b) the US President.
   c) large US industries.

2. OSHA success stories include...

   a) saving thousands of lives in the workplace.
   b) stopping a serious lung disease that made clothing workers sick.
   c) reducing the number of workers hurt in certain industries.
   d) a and b.
   e) all of the above.

3. How do employers benefit from safe and healthy work conditions?

   a) Workers are sick less and so they miss fewer days of work.
   b) Workers complain more about the work conditions.
   c) The workplace becomes more productive.
   d) a and b.   e) a and c.

Context Clues

Below is a paragraph from the article about work safety organizations. Some of the words have been removed. Complete the paragraph by using words from the list below. Try not to look back at the article.

eliminated	contact
success	industries
accidents	workplace
history	complaint

OSHA was created by the US Congress and has had many 1. _____

stories in its 30-year 2. _____ . For example, since 1970 the number of

deaths in the 3. _____ has been cut by 74%. OSHA has fought for laws

that have almost 4. _____ brown lung disease--a serious disease that can

both disable and kill--in the clothing industry. 5. _____ and illnesses are

usually much lower in 6. _____ where OSHA has been able to concentrate

its attention. If you have a 7. _____ or a question about your workplace

conditions, you can 8. _____ your local OSHA office.

Discussion Questions

1. When you do the same movement on a job day after day, you may get what is called a repetitive motion injury. One of the most common is called Carpal Tunnel Syndrome. People who work with computers sometimes suffer from this condition. List some other occupations were repetitive motion injury could occur.

2. Some groups and politicians say we do not know enough about repetitive motion injuries to make laws to prevent them. Do you think a law is needed to help workers with this condition? Why or why not?

Air Travel Safety

Millions of people travel by airplane every year. Most of the time, traveling by air is much safer than traveling by automobile. The chances of a serious accident while flying are very small. Still, at the beginning of your flight take a few minutes and listen closely to the aircrew as they explain emergency procedures.

After you have heard the safety procedures told to you, there is usually a card in the seat pocket with the same information written on it about how to find the exits and how to open the plane's doors. You can read this card to make sure you understand what to do if the plane gets into trouble. If you are still unsure as to what you should do, ask a crew member to explain it to you again.

Of course, in the event of a real emergency people need to move quickly and calmly, so it is prudent to know where the nearest exit is located. It is also wise to know what to do if the airplane fills with smoke or loses oxygen. You should also practice fastening and unfastening your seatbelt because in an emergency you may have to do it without being able to see.

Sometimes, a fire might start on the plane. The crew will attempt to put it out, but smoke can cause breathing problems. During a fire passengers should get their heads down as low as possible. If a fire breaks out, passengers might find breathing easier if they put a cloth over their mouths.

Another problem may be an airplane that loses oxygen. If this emergency occurs, oxygen masks will come down from the ceiling. Put the mask on, stay sitting down and be prepared for the plane to descend quickly because the pilot will try to bring the plane lower so the passengers can breathe normally.

Sit back and enjoy your flight!

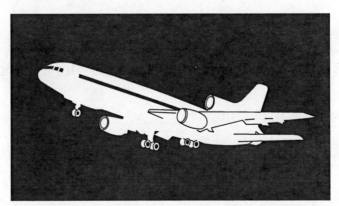

Multiple Choice

1. Flying is _____ driving.

   a) more dangerous than
   b) as safe as
   c) safer than
   d) none of these

2. If you do not understand safety procedures after hearing them and reading about them, you should...

   a) forget about them.   b) tell a crew member.   c) visit the pilot.   d) find the nearest exit.

3. If the airplane loses oxygen, you should sit down because...

   a) the plane may descend quickly.   b) it is more comfortable.   c) it is easier to breathe.

Context Clues

Below is a paragraph from the article about air travel safety. Some of the words have been removed. Complete the paragraph by using words from the list below. Try not to look back at the article.

flight	closely
safer	traveling
millions	procedures
aircrew	serious

1. _____ of people travel by airplane every year. Most of the time,

2. _____ by air is much 3. _____ than traveling by

automobile. The chances of a 4. _____ accident while flying are very

small. Still, at the beginning of your 5. _____ take a few minutes and

listen 6. _____ to the 7. _____ as they explain

emergency 8. _____.

Problems And Solutions

Complete each sentence below.

1. You should cover your mouth with a cloth and move your head as low as possible.

   The problem is _____.

2. The plane is losing oxygen.

   The solution is _____.

Answer Key

Page 1   **INSECT BITES**
Multiple Choice
1. c
2. c
3. c
Sentence Completions
1. wash the area with soap and water.
2. that there are more than 2 million different kinds of insects.
Common And Proper Nouns
common nouns
(there are many more)
humans, insects, diseases, ticks, scientists, soap, rash
proper nouns
West Nile, Malaria, Lyme

Page 3   **PERSONAL INFORMATION**
Multiple Choice
1. c
Sentence Completions
1. the person can steal your money.
2. finding out confidential information about you.
3. call the police.
Related Words
1. know
2. information
3. personal
4. careful
5. criminal
Adverbs
1. just
2. too
3. very
4. normally
5. also
6. even
7. immediately

Page 5   **A.I.D.S. / H.I.V.**
Multiple Choice
1. b
2. c
3. c
Summarizing Information
1. e
2. c
3. a
4. f

Answer Key

Page 7   ASTHMA AND CHILDREN
Multiple Choice
1. c
2. a
3. c
Synonyms or Antonyms?
1. synonym
2. synonym
3. antonym
4. synonym
5. antonym
Discussion Question
No one knows exactly why the number of asthma cases are increasing, but some have pointed to environmental concerns--for example, the increase of pollutants in the air--as one reason.

Page 9   DRINKING WATER SAFETY
Multiple Choice
1. c
2. a
3. c
5 Ways to Make Water Safer
1. Test the water for lead.
2. Listen for advisories about drinking water.
3. Filter the water.
4. Boil the water.
5. Avoid drinking water that smells strange or is cloudy.
4 Words with Z sound
(there are others)
Nowadays, viruses, problems, days

Page 11   BICYCLES
Multiple Choice
1. c
2. b
3. a
Vocabulary
1. c
2. a
3. d
4. e
5. b
Statistics
1. 70%
2. 85%
3. 15-20%
4. 39%
5. 80%

Answer Key

Page 13   **CHOKING**

Multiple Choice

1. c
2. b
3. d

Vocabulary Activity

Dangerous Foods: hot dogs, nuts, large pieces of meat or cheese, whole grapes, hard or sticky candy, popcorn, raw carrots

Dangerous Household Items: marbles, pen or marker caps, batteries, small toy parts, balloons, coins

Dangerous Actions: not chewing food thoroughly, eating food while walking around, not cutting food into small pieces, eating food while laying down

Page 15   **911**

Multiple Choice

1. b
2. c
3. d

Noun/Verb

1. Noun
2. Verb
3. Verb
4. Noun

Page 17   **EARTHQUAKES**

Multiple Choice

1. c
2. a
3. b

True or False?

1. T
2. T
3. F
4. F
5. T

Answer Key

Page 19   ELECTRICAL FIRES
Multiple Choice
1. a and c
2. c
3. b
Vocabulary
1. iron
2. toaster
3. microwave
Summarizing Information
1. c
2. f
3. d
4. e

Page 21   SMOKE ALARMS
Multiple Choice
1. b
2. c
3. b
Sentence Completions
1. have alarms that do not work.
2. in minutes.
3. they are asleep when the fire starts.
4. bedroom and hallway.
Homophones
1. "dye" should be "die"
2. "no" should be "know"
3. "too" should be "to"
4. "week" should be "weak"
5. "won" should be "one"

Answer Key

Page 23   FIRST AID KITS

Multiple Choice

1. b
2. a
3. c
4. c

Matching

1. c
2. a
3. d
4. e
5. b

Misspelled Words

1. common
2. supplies
3. individually
4. bleeding
5. applying
6. different
7. bottle
8. hopefully.

Add a double letter which had been left out.

Page 25   FAINTING AND FEVER

Multiple Choice

1. c
2. a
3. d

Vocabulary

1. breathing is not a part of the body
2. body is not a medical condition
3. sometimes is not a common occurence
4. reaction does not involve a physical place or moving something physically

Definition

1. A symptom is sign or indication of an illness.

Answer Key

Page 27   CAR PASSENGER SAFETY

Multiple Choice

1. b
2. a
3. b

Find the Opposite

1. die
2. simple
3. front
4. drunk
5. hard

Find The Mistakes

1. Small children should have special seats.
2. Adults should wear seat belts.
3. It is safer to walk than to ride with a driver who is drunk.

Page 29   FUN IN THE SUN

Multiple Choice

1. d
2. e
3. c

Matching

1. c
2. a
3. b

Page 31   COMMUNICABLE DISEASES

Multiple Choice

1. d
2. a
3. b

Error Correction

1. "unhealthy" should be "healthy"
2. "good" should be "not good"
3. "are" should be "are not"
4. "benefit" should be "risk" or "benefit" should be "not a benefit"

Building Words

1. communicable
2. diseases
3. antibiotic
4. careful
5. uncooked

Answer Key

Page 33   HALLOWEEN SAFETY
Multiple Choice
1. d
2. c
3. a
Jack-o'-Lanterns
1. pumpkins
2. candle
3. Jack/hell/lantern

Page 35   AVOIDING VICTIMIZATION
Multiple Choice
1. d
2. b
3. b
Word Endings
1. criminal
2. surroundings
3. pedestrian
Infinitives
to stay, to go, to attack, to use, to arrange

Page 37   CHRISTMASTIME SAFETY
Multiple Choice
1. d
2. b
3. c
Correct the Mistake
1. "Always" should be "Never": Never use candles as decorations on Christmas trees.
2. "month" should be "year": Christmas trees cause hundreds of fires each year.
3. "Real" should be "Artificial" and "artificial" should be "real": Artificial trees are safer and cleaner than real trees.
4. "week" should be "day": If you buy a real Christmas tree, you should water it at least once a day.
5. "sink" should be "stand": Make sure you place the tree in a stand that is strong enough to hold it.

Page 39   DRUG AND VITAMIN LABELS
Multiple Choice
1. a
2. d
3. c
Correct the Mistakes
1. "friend" should be "doctor"
2. "ignore" should be "do not ignore"
3. "receipt" should be "label"
4. "more strict" should be"not as strict"

Answer Key

Page 41   MYTHS ABOUT SEAT BELTS
Multiple Choice
1. a
2. c
3. b
The Main Idea
b

Page 43   SAFETY FOR DISABLED PEOPLE
Multiple Choice
1. b
2. c
3. b
Finding Examples
1. walking up stairs, crossing the street, getting in or out of vehicles or buildings
2. special parking spaces; special seats on trains, buses and subways; ramps
Adjectives
1. disabled
2. special
3. large
4. unauthorized
5. accessible
6. public
7. dangerous
8. impossible
9. careful
10. obvious

Page 45   PLAYGROUNDS
Multiple Choice
1. a
2. b
3. c
Match the Sentence Parts
1. c
2. d
3. b
4. a
Statistics
1. 70%
2. over 200,000
3. every two-and-a-half minutes
4. 11%

Answer Key

Page 47 SCHOOL SAFETY
Multiple Choice
1. c
2. a
3. c
Details
1. taking an interest in the child's life and being involved in the child's school.
2. Sharing a student schedule with parents and friends.
Apostrophe
1. If parents notice a sudden change in their child's behavior, they should investigate.
2. Parents need to be observant of their children's behavior.
3. Parents should be involved in their children's school.

Page 49 PROTECTING YOUR EARS
Multiple Choice
1. b
2. c
3. a
Vocabulary
1. replaced
2. tweezers
3. tip
4. elbow
5. pair

Page 51 ANIMAL BITES
Multiple Choice
1. b
2. b
3. d
Finding Details
1. make loud sounds, touch the animal
2. foam at the mouth, attack for no reason.
And, Or, But
1. It may also show its teeth, bend its ears back, and tighten its muscles.
2. An animal is more likely to bite if it has just given birth or if it is injured.
3. I like dogs but I do not like cats.

Answer Key

Page 53   PROTECTING YOUR EYES
Multiple Choice
1. b
2. e
3. d

True or False?
1. FALSE. Although carrots have a lot of Vitamin A, which is a necessary vitamin for sight, you only need a very small amount of it for good eyesight.
2. FALSE. Eye glasses can help you see better, but if you do not use them your eyes will not be hurt.
3. FALSE. Everyone should have a regular eye examination, whether they are having problems or not.
4. FALSE. Although reading in poor light can make your eyes tired, it will not hurt your eyes.
5. FALSE. Regular eye examinations and using the proper eye protection can help prevent the loss of your eyesight.

Synonyms Or Antonyms?
1. antonym
2. synonym
3. antonym
4. antonym
5. synonym

Page 55   FIRE EXITS
Multiple Choice
1. d
2. a
3. c

Opposites
1. exit
2. remember
3. strange
4. destroy
5. block

Page 57   POISONING
Multiple Choice
1. c
2. c
3. d

Match the Sentence Parts
1. b
2. d
3. c
4. a

Summarizing Information
1. f
2. c
3. a
4. e

Answer Key

Page 59   PEDESTRIAN SAFETY
Multiple Choice
1. c
2. a
3. c
Imperatives
(there are several: some examples are:)
1. Remember to ask. 2. Be aware of plants. 3. Understand that larger vehicles...
Bad Advice
1. Walk facing the traffic so you can see the traffic.
2. Use a flashlight so cars can see you walking.
3. Use a sidewalk when it is possible.

Page 61   STRESS
Multiple Choice
1. d
2. b
3. c
Vocabulary Activity
Symptoms of Stress: lower back pain, gained a lot of weight, diarrhea, frequent headaches, trouble sleeping, trouble concentrating
Why Stress Happens: being hurried, driving in heavy traffic, doing poorly in school, breaking up with a boy or girlfriend
Possible Remedies: meditation, find time to relax, drink less coffee, playing a sport, eating right

Page 63   VISITING A DOCTOR
Multiple Choice
1. c
2. c
3. b
Mistakes
1. tell his doctor about his allergies.
2. ask her doctor about her medicine.
3. honest with the doctor.
Your & Their
1. You should be certain to understand your doctor's instructions
2. Doctors want to help their patients
3. He will explain your condition.
4. Doctors need your help to do their job properly

Answer Key

Page 65   THE ABCs of FIRE EXTINGUISHERS
Multiple Choice
1. e
2. b
3. c
What is the Right Order?
6-2-4-3-5-7-1
Summarizing Information
1. a
2. f
3. d
4. c
Related Activity
Possible answers: Your local fire department, your ocal library, the Internet.

Page 67   DROWNING PREVENTION
Multiple Choice
1. b
2. c
3. a
Definitions
1. drown
2. life jacket
 3. floating or changing strokes
Minimal Pairs
1. "like" should be "lake"
2. "fill" should be "fall"
3. "racks" should be "rocks"
4. "deer" should be "deep"
 5."fan" should be "fun"

Page 69   TORNADOES
Multiple Choice
1. b
2. c
3. b
Correct the Mistakes
1. In January 1974, a tornado in McComb, Mississippi picked up three school buses and threw them over an eight-foot wall.
2. An unusually strong tornado in Birmingham, Alabama in 1998 picked up things that were carried over 100 miles before they fell to the ground.
3. Most tornadoes last less than an hour, but some can last several hours.
4. Tornadoes have wind speeds that can be more than 200 miles per hour (321 kilometers per hour).
5. If a tornado is near you, you should not go to places that have large roofs, like cafeterias, auditoriums and gymnasiums.
6. If it is possible, try to sit under a heavy piece of furniture, like a table or desk.

Answer Key

Page 71   **AUTOMOBILE MAINTENANCE**

Multiple Choice

1. d
2. b
3. a

Matching

1. d
2. c
3. b
4. a

Quantifiers

1. more
2. some
3. at least
4. many
5. enough
6. both

Page 73   **THE FIGHT AGAINST CANCER**

Multiple Choice

1. c
2. a
3. a

Match the Sentence Parts

1. b
2. d
3. c
4. a

Summarizing Information

1. e
2. d
3. f
4. b

The Main Idea

b

Answer Key

Page 75   DEALING WITH THE POLICE
Multiple Choice
1. c
2. a
3. c

Sentence Completion
1. hurt or injure you
2. follow
3. a lawyer

Do/Does
1. Do not shout at the police and threaten them.
2. Do not make quick or sudden movements.
3. A police officer does not want to hurt you.
4. A police officer does not want to let the bad guys get away.
5. Do not hit a police officer.

Page 77   THE HEIMLICH MANEUVER
Multiple Choice
1. b
2. a
3. c

Summarizing Information
1. d
2. a
3. b
4. e

page 79   PRODUCT LABELS AND EXPIRATION DATES
Multiple Choice
1. c
2. e

Finding Examples
(there are many more)
1. most soft drinks
2. most chocolate
3. most coffee.

It
It as a subject (there are many more)
1. It is always a good idea to know how fresh the products are when you buy them...
2. For example, if a product's expiration date is January 5, it should not be consumed on January 6.
It as an object (there are many more)
1. Before you cook meat or fish, or drink milk, be sure that it smells the way it should and that its color is normal.
2. If meat is not wrapped tightly or if a milk carton is open, do not buy it.

Answer Key

Page 81   THE INTERNET
Multiple Choice
1. c
2. b
3. a and c
Vocabulary of the Internet
1. b
2. d
3. a
4. c

Page 83   BOATING SAFETY
Multiple Choice
1. c
2. b
Sentence Completions
1. more accidents occur when boaters drink.
2. they can get help if you need it.
3. they need to know about changing weather conditions.
Commands
1. Take a radio and extra batteries.
2. Do not operate a boat when you drink alcohol.
3. Learn the province's boating laws.

Page 85   TIPS FOR BABYSITTERS
Multiple Choice
1. b
2. c
3. a
Summarizing Information
1. c
2. e
3. d
4. a
Related Activities
1. The house phone number, the number where the parents can be reached, the number of a close friend or relative, the number of the family doctor, the number of the poison control center and, of course, the number of emergencies: 911.

Answer Key

Page 87   IMMUNIZATIONS
Multiple Choice
1. d
2. c
3. c
Remembering Details
(there are many more)
polio, mumps, measles
Corrections
1. "ignore" should be "understand"
2. "fun" should be "health"
3. "want" should be "need"
4. "unneeded" should be "needed"
5. "colds" should be "mumps"

Page 89   THE SCHOOL BUS
Multiple Choice
1. a
2. c
3. b
Matching the Numbers
1. b
2. c
3. a
4. d
Summarizing Information
1. e
2. d
3. c
4. f

Page 91   SWIMMING POOL SAFETY
Multiple Choice
1. b
2. b
3. d
Vocabulary
1. c
2. d
3. b
4. a
Summarizing Information
1. c
2. g
3. f
4. d
5. a

116

Answer Key

Page 93   FROSTBITE
Multiple Choice
1. b
2. a
3. c
Correct the Mistake
1. One warning sign of frostbite is when your skin becomes red or very white.
2. Frostbite can usually be prevented if the right steps are taken before going outside.
3. Cream or rubbing oil can be used to protect the face.
4. Even though they are dressed properly, children may still have problems with the cold if they are inactive for a long time.
The Main Idea
a

Page 95   EMERGENCY EVACUATION PROCEDURES
Multiple Choice
1. b
2. c
3. a

Page 97   WORK SAFETY ORGANIZATIONS
Multiple Choice
1. a
2. e
3. e
Context Clues
1. success
2. history
3. workplace
4. eliminated
5. accidents
6. industries
7. complaint
8. contact

Answer Key

Page 99   AIR TRAVEL SAFETY

Multiple Choice

1. c
2. b
3. a

Context Clues

1. millions
2. traveling
3. safer
4. serious
5. flight
6. closely
7. aircrew
8. procedures

Problems and Solutions

1. a fire on the plane.
2. put on your oxygen mask.